Quickiez Online:

The First Anthology

The Niftian

Quickiez Online: The First Anthology

By The Niftian

ISBN 978-1-105-44324-4

http://www.QuickiezOnline.com

Table of Contents

The First Quickie ____ 6

The Coffeehouse ____ 7

Office Sex, pt 1 ____ 11

Office Sex, pt 2 ____ 14

Meet Me In The Shower ____ 17

The Ultimate Sex Story, pt 1.5 ____ 19

The Ultimate Sex Story, pt 2 ____ 21

Give Thanks ____ 24

The Ultimate Sex Story, pt 3 ____ 29

The Ultimate Sex Story, pt 4 ____ 31

The Ultimate Sex Story, pt 5 (FINALE) ____ 32

Passion, pt 1 ____ 35

Passion, pt 2 ____ 37

First Date Sex, pt 1 ____ 39

First Date Sex, pt 2 ____ 42

First Date Sex, pt 3 ____ 44

Car Sexin' ____ 46

Mile High ____ 48

Do It Like It's The First Time, pt 1 ____ 52

Do It Like It's The First Time, pt 2 ____ 54

The Head Nurse ____ 57

Lunchtime Special ____ 58

Putting In Work ____ 61

Fantasy ____ 63

Whip Me, Strip Me, pt 1 ____ 64

Whip Me, Strip Me, pt 2 66
Night of Debauchery, pt 1 69
Night of Debauchery, pt 2 (The Revenge) 71
Our Mamasita 74
The Backdoor 76
About The Author *79*
Connect with The Niftian Online: 79

The First Quickie

Come in. Hurry! My day was hard and long, just like the manhood in my pants that is eager to be inside you. As soon as you cross the threshold of my house, we are eagerly pulling clothes off of each other: jacket, shirt, blouse, pants, shoes getting kicked, buttons getting popped. I don't care, and neither do you: we'll buy new ones later.

I kiss you swiftly, tasting the frustration from your stressful day and getting even more turned on at the thought of relieving you of it. You thrust your tongue in my mouth, probing my passion while pushing me to the couch in the far corner of the living room.

Within moments, you are straddling me and because of our excitement, I enter you easily. A soft moan escapes your lips as you press the soft skin of your face against mine. Your arms are wrapped around my neck as you glide up and down on my shaft. My arms are hugging you, loving the feel of your ribs against my biceps.

I flex my thighs, pushing myself deeper and deeper into you, soliciting a loud gasp right by my ear. I love it. I tug lightly on your hair, pulling your head back so that I have access to your beautiful neck. I lick slowly from one side to the other, taking nibbles along the way. The sensation in my lap of your pussy getting wetter and wetter on me elicit moans from my lips. I can hear the love sounds we're making.

You lean forward, raising your ass up to a point where the tip of my penis is barely inside you. You maneuver yourself so that you can turn around facing away from me and giving me a beautiful view of your full, sexy ass. You place your hands on my knees and continue to ride me, placing me as deep inside you as your body allows.

You turn your head slightly so that you can face me. You're gorgeous. You speed up the tempo, my dick pounding in and out of you. You arch your back and throw your head back, ecstasy rocking your very being. The sight of you reaching a climax, and the sight of your juices coating my stiff cock sends me over the edge. We cum together, our juices mingling with each other in a cocktail of passion, lust and love.

As our desires slowly subside, you lean back against me, turning your head to kiss me with the kisses of your mouth. Mmmm...I feel my erection growing again.

The Coffeehouse

A coffeehouse: dimly lit, and with sparse furniture. A couch here, a love seat there, a few over-sized and overstuffed ottomans. A nifty little bar. A stage for karaoke night. It's fairly small and quaint, but it's the fulfillment of a dream, and it's actually fairly popular, growing more and more so as the months go on. Paintings from local artists adorn the walls, along with pictures of some of the regulars. It's a great spot to come to and has gained a reputation as a "cute little couple's spot" because of the Sunday Slow Sessions. That's when the old jukebox in the corner gets preset to nothing but old school jams. The Chi-Lites come through, Smokey Robinson breezes in on a quiet storm, The Temptations make you remember why she's your girl, and The Stylistics cause you to make up after that trifling little breakup over nothing.

Sundays always turn me on because the customers can be seen getting closer and closer as the evening wears on, and you can see the gears in their heads turning. I like to imagine what they're saying to each other in betwixt the verses on the songs. Mr. and Mrs. Robinson are probably snickering over making love in the living room now that the oldest child is off to college. Ms. Jones definitely has a thing going on with Willie James, and she doesn't care who thinks it's wrong, as long as he uses that tongue that he's famed for in some circles. Sam Matthews lays in wait in the corner, peering over his tall glass, probing the minds of the guests just like I am. I wonder if that is all Sam thinks on...

"The time has come, the walrus said, for me to close up shop!" I announce the last call in my familiar fashion while absently thinking of what lonely chick flick I'll fall asleep to tonight. I opened this place up with my own money and with my own time and energy, and that never left much time for dating. So here I am: a lonely, bored female in my late 20s with no social life outside of here at the shop. That's ok to me though, my customers provide me with more than enough excitement.

After the last of my customers has left and I have locked up behind them, I turn back towards finishing my closing duties and jump, startled. Sam Matthews is leaning against the bar, turning up the very last of his drink.

"Sam, what the hell?! What are you doing here? I'm closed, baby, and you gotta' go." I turn around to unlock the door when his voice stops me in my tracks. A deep, rumbling voice. Barry White-ish, I'd call it. Sam never talked much except to order his drink, and when he did, you didn't catch the full effect of it because there was so much background noise. This time however, it was just he and I.

"Don't do that, Marylin. It's been a long time that I've been thinking about you, and I think I finally got the heart to say something about it." Without knowing it was happening, I realized that my panties were wet, soaked even. I'd never heard that much out of Sam, and the fact that he was talking about me turned me on some kind of bad! See, Sam wasn't just a smooth talker. He was also a very sexy brother. He lost his wife some years ago, I heard, so many women were shy to approach him. That, and the fact that he generally kept to himself. There were many that tried, though. Sam Matthews was tall, 6 foot and more, and had the prettiest brown skin. He kept his appearance neat, and you could tell he ate well and worked out in some fashion or another, because he was wearing that muscle on his frame very well. Shit, I admit that even I daydreamed about Sam once or twice. I wonder if he played ball in school?

This whole time I was in a daze and Sam was walking closer to me. He'd been thinking about me a long time? When's the first time I thought about him? It was a long time ago. Then I wondered, when was the last time I was with a man? I pushed that thought out of my head: way too long was the answer. I looked up into Sam's deep, dark eyes and I was amazed at what I saw: loneliness, and yet so much passion. I was touched, because I could see then that he wanted to share all of that with me. No more words needed to be exchanged.

I wrapped my hands around the back of his neck and pulled him down to me, showing him the passion in my kisses. I hoped for the briefest moment that I wasn't being too forward, and then I remembered: Sam approached ME. So fuck it, let's do this. Birds of a feather clearly think alike because no sooner had the thought formed in my mind than Sam effortlessly pick me up, carrying me over to the couch on the other side of the bar. I was amazed at his strength. Don't get it twisted: I am in no way a big woman. But still, the fact that he carried my 135 pound frame all the way across the room like I was a child turned me ON! Ooh, and he was so gentle. He placed me down with as much ease as he had picked me up, and not once did we break our kiss. I started to unbutton his shirt, starting at the neck and feverishly working my way down. I was horny, and I was going to fuck the shit out of this tall drink of a man! Sam, however, was more refined, bless his heart. He slowly undid my blouse, easily unbuttoned my jeans, carefully slid off my shoes, skillfully undid my bra, and then broke that sweet kiss. I was hungry with desire at this point, and yet Sam seemed so in control of his senses. Of course, that only turned me on even more.

At this point, I'm naked save for my panties by my girl Vickie, and Sam is still completely dressed! I didn't even get his shirt all the way off. I giggle silently and lean back while he undresses. I never thought I'd see the day when all of this sexiness would stand before me. This. Is going. To be. Fun.

After what felt like hours, Sam was completely nude in front of me, and damn! Clearly, this man was sent from the heavens and was a fallen angel or something! His pecs were so massive and well defined, right along with his abs. One, two, three, four, five, six of them! Yes! Every single muscle could be seen, and then there was the one that I really cared about. "Damn...!" I could hear Sam's deep chuckle above me. I didn't mean to say that out loud.

"Marylin, I've wanted you for so long, to taste you, to feel you, and to please you. May I, please?" The look in his eyes was genuine and there was no way that I could, or would, say no. I nodded my silent agreement and then watched as he slowly, painstakingly slowly, pulled my panties down my thighs and calves and around my ankles. He licked his lips. I could just imagine the wonders that tongue could accomplish, but that would have to wait. I was an empty vessel and I needed to be filled. If he did all that he should right now, then there would be plenty to eat later. I spread myself open to him and placed my feet behind his back and above his ass, pulling his huge and erect dick towards me.

Like I said, it has been some time since I've gotten any action, let alone any good action, so once the tip of his dick met my pussy, I came. I'm not even embarrassed to admit it. It was so big, and I knew that I was going to be so tight; how in the hell would all of that man meat fit inside me?! Fuck it, I was going to find out. I reached down and, using my hands, spread my pussy open for him, feeling my juices coating my fingers. I ran my fingertips along the side of his dick as he slowly worked his way inside me. Like a pro, he knew better than to force it all in at once. He went in two inches, then slid it back out, went in four inches, then slid it back out, went in six inches and back out again. He did this over and over until all of Sam was inside of me. It was glorious! I felt his balls, large and heavy, against my ass as he leaned over me. I leaned forward, kissing his chest, sucking on his nipples and feeling my own become as hard as the dick that was inside me.

I was in heaven. Everything about this man was calm, paced, serene and intentional. Most guys would be fucking me like a damned rabbit and busting a nut all over my stomach, but that's not what Sam wanted, and not what either of us needed. I looked up, surprised to see him gazing into my eyes. To think, I'd be on my way home right now, thinking over my Sex and The City DVDs if I'd have kicked Sam out. Instead, this man was here, making love to me and making my pussy scream. Ah, the things life throws at you. I loved the pace he was putting up, because it helped me get accustomed to his huge shaft. But I was at that point. You know that point: where the love-making is nice, but you want to get fucked. I reached around, grabbed his ass on the out stroke and squeezed, slamming his dick into me, right up to the hilt. I cried in ecstasy, not realizing that I was coming again, for what seemed like the millionth time.

Sam knew I wasn't in pain, and also knew that that's exactly what I wanted. So he drilled me, over and over again, my juices making the process so easy for him, because I had cum and pussy juice all over his dick. I wonder: can I really handle that much dick in me? I decided to give it the ol' college try and motioned for Sam to sit on the couch so I could straddle him. As I got myself in position, he took my right nipple in his mouth, causing wave after wave of orgasms to go crashing through my body. I love it, oh god, I loved it. I reached behind me and placed that shaft in the perfect position to enter me again and sat down on it. Allllll the way down on it, and that was a long way to go. In this position, his dick hit a spot that I didn't even know existed, and it seems that I caught him by surprise as well because he paused on massaging my breasts and sucking my nipples and gasped, his eyes rolling in the back of his head. Ooh, I still had it!

I knew that Sam couldn't take much more of this, and I wanted to give him just as much as he'd given me, so I picked up the tempo. I slid my pussy back and forth in his lap, his dick hitting my g-spot with each thrust and then I jumped up and down on him, causing my breasts to fly in his face. I could tell he loved it, and I could tell he was close to busting one hellified nut.

"Oooooohhh!!!" was all that escaped from his mouth as he crossed that sexual threshold. I jumped off of his dick even though I didn't want to. I wanted to taste all of him, and now! I placed my face right in front of his shaft and started stroking his dick for all I was worth. It wasn't until I placed my tongue on the tip of him that he erupted, and I caught every ounce that I could. Either he hadn't cum in eons or he naturally busts a lot. I took in what I could and made sure to clean up the rest.

"Damn, I haven't experienced that in so long," he said, after catching his breath and coming back down to earth.

"Me either," I replied. "And we're not done," I said as I pulled on my pants. "This Sunday is still very young." I pulled him off the couch, enjoying the strong, warm embrace he gave me, followed by kisses to my forehead, cheeks and lips. I glided over to the jukebox, cutting Lenny Williams off and turned around, admiring Sam as he got dressed. The only question was where would we wake up on Monday morning, his place or mine? Oh, this is one Sunday Slow Session I will definitely not forget.

Office Sex, pt 1

I knew I was wrong. Well, I think I was wrong. You'd probably think I was wrong. If anyone else that worked here knew, they'd think I was wrong. They'd say "David Marcel West, you are wrong!" Well no, maybe SHE is wrong. 'She' is my boss: Sandra Moore, Assistant CFO of a Fortune 1000 Company based here in Richmond. She is the epitome of success, determination, drive and she had the heart to do her job and to do it well. That is what attracts me to her. That and the fact that she is the sexiest 34 year old woman I know. She worked so hard to get where she is and to get there as early as she did, but it didn't show in her features. A lot of her peers looked drained, over worked and miserable. That and they were mostly old white men in their 60s. Sandra, on the other hand, looked powerful, sexy, confident and fierce.

Ms. Moore, as I called her, always found the time to keep her body in shape. She worked out at the gym we had in the lowest levels of the building that the company built for the employees but that so few took advantage of. She had the most impressive body, and always wore the most sophisticated outfits to show off her assets, but without looking trashy. I loved her class.

I don't know what it was that made Sandra Moore approach me the way she did. I had been working for her for a few months and loving the opportunity to learn about the industry. She warned me during the interview process that the job called for long hours, late nights and a lot of dedication. I was committed. I wanted this and truth be told, I wanted her. However, I filed that under 'schoolboy fantasy' and went about my work, striving to prove to her that I was a sound investment and could be a very positive asset to the company.

It wasn't long before I learned about those late nights. The work could be boring at times, and it provided us with ample opportunity to learn about each other and talk of all sorts of non work related stuff. It was on one such evening about two months ago that she made her move.

"So, David, your girlfriend hasn't started worrying you about your work schedule?" A simple ploy for information. I know this now, but I didn't see it then.

"No, ma'am; no girlfriend to worry about such issues" was my reply. It was true, too. I hadn't had a girlfriend in over a year and hadn't gotten laid in almost that long, either. I wasn't as good with the ladies as my friends were. "And at this rate, I won't have one anytime soon." I tried to shrug it off with laughter.

"Damn. Even I find the time for some fun. You just have to learn how to balance it all," she said as she sat down on her desk in front of me. Lucky desk. "For example, I make time for the gym at least three times a week and I cannot go more than two weeks without getting my pussy eaten." I almost fell out of the chair I was sitting in. I knew Sandra Moore spoke her mind, but I wasn't expecting this! Clearly she knew she caught me off guard, because she started laughing. "David, do you find me attractive?"

"Y-y-yes?" That was all I could say. What was happening here? It was one thing for Ms. Moore to be sitting so close to me, her Body by Victoria's Secret invading my nostrils, but it was another thing entirely for her to be sharing details of her sex life with me. And now she was unbuttoning her blouse! Yea, I was about to pass out. "Ms. Moore, what are you...?"

She cut me off. "If you're offended, tell me, and we'll forever act as if you're not staring at my breasts right now. If you're not, then you are about to eat my pussy. It's been over my two week limit and I am a fiend right now. You look like you're in shape and can handle yourself, and me. Can you?"

My brain was locked. I didn't know what to say. So I didn't say anything. I just helped her out of her slacks and panties, slid my chair forward and gave myself a mental high five for the way this night was turning out. I could see the juices from her pussy glistening in the dimly lit room and I could smell the fragrance of her body around me. Her essence smelled so sweet. I couldn't wait to taste it.

"David, this is going to have to be our little secret, do you understand?" I nodded my affirmation, still transfixed by the way she made her pussy wink at me. I was so hungry. I leaned forward, my tongue out, and placed as much as that sweet nectar in my mouth as I could. My tongue slid inside her wet slit easily, and my nose nuzzled perfectly against her hard clit. Wow, she looked good, smelled divine, and tasted GREAT! I was not on the 18th floor of an office building right now; I was in heaven. It had been a very long time since I tasted some grade-A pussy but I must have been doing something right, because Ms. Moore was running her perfectly manicured nails across my scalp, and that drove me wild. I licked her kitty for all I was worth, humming on her clit, kind of like a vibrator.

"Oh!" She really dug that, I could see. This was a perfect picture: her legs across my shoulders and around my neck, her hands all over my head and my hands reaching up, massaging her perfect 34DD breasts. This moment could not have been any more perfect. She started slow grinding her pussy into my face and I had her juices all over my mouth, cheeks, nose and eyes. I couldn't get enough. I heard her purr turn into a growl and her legs tightened around my neck. This queen was about to bless me with her cum, I could tell. She let out a shriek unlike anything I'd heard before in my 22 years and her pussy exploded! I'd heard stories about women that could ejaculate, but I'd never seen it for myself. I was amazed. She tasted so sweet, like honeysuckle and cherries. I drank every single drop that her body gave me, clutching her left breast in one hand and her right thigh in the other. I didn't want this to end.

"Fuck me, David, now!" I looked up, and could barely make out her almond shaped eyes in the dim light. Her tone was authoritative, but her expression was pleading. Sweet. I stood up and quickly danced my way out of my pants and boxers, not even bothering to undo my shirt or tie. My penis stood at attention, vibrating at the entrance to her pussy. Ms. Moore placed her legs around me again, this time behind my back, and pulled me into her, my dick sliding in effortlessly because her pussy was still dripping wet from her cum. I moaned loudly; I couldn't help it. Not only had it been a very long time since I'd gotten any, but I'd NEVER had any pussy like this. I buried my face in her neck and hair, inhaling her essence while I started stroking inside her for all I was worth. I knew I was packing with something, and I wanted her to feel every single inch of it. I felt my balls slapping against her perineum as I drilled myself into her, loving the sound her pussy made while it sucked on my dick.

I'm not really into the pain thing, but the way she was scratching my back had me over the edge. I took my left hand and wrapped it in her hair, pulling on it and loving the moan that escaped her lips. "YES" was all that she said. She was enjoying this: good. I leaned back and placed her calves over my shoulders, causing her to lie down on her desk. I pulled her towards me just enough to cause that voluptuous ass to hang over the desk so my nuts could slap against her ass while I fucked her with everything I had. I looked down at her and loved the way her breasts were rocking on her chest. She caught my eyes and grabbed her chest, bringing each tit up to suck on her nipples, one at a time. Damn. I'd never been with a woman who had boobs big enough to do that, and Ms. Moore's rack was perfect!

I could feel my balls swelling, and I knew that feeling all too well: I was about to bust. I wanted to hold on for hours, but the sensation wouldn't go away. I tried slowing down, but Ms. Moore wasn't having any of that.

"I don't care if you cum; I'll suck your dick until you're hard again! Now, FUCK ME!" Well shit, ok. She spread her legs wide for me, opening her pussy in the process. I leaned forward, continuing to piston in and out of her eternally wet pussy while sucking on her nipples, enjoying her chocolate taste. I could feel cum racing up my shaft and I was powerless to stop it. Ms. Moore furthered matters by squeezing her pussy lips tighter and tighter around me. Oh, god! The whole scene was just too much! I pulled out at the last possible moment, nearly passing out as ounce after ounce of cum erupted from my dick, spraying Ms. Sandra Moore in all of her sexy glory. I couldn't help but to fall back into my seat and watch Ms. Moore jump up and start to suck the remnants of my seed out of my shaft. I'd NEVER experienced this before. It felt as if I was having another orgasm!

"Ms. Mooooooooore!" My eyes were forced shut and all I could see were yellow stars, purple moons and green clovers. Either I was having one hellacious trip or I was in a XXX rated Lucky Charms commercial. Amazingly enough, my dick was still rock hard, even as Ms. Moore drained the very last drop of cum out of me.

"Mmmm...I don't think you're done yet, big boy. What do you think, is it quitting time David?" I didn't even respond. I pulled Ms. Moore's head back and kissed her firmly on the lips. Then I stood up, bringing her with me. I turned her around and bent her over the desk. This was going to be a very long night indeed, and I was DEFINITELY going to put in work.

Office Sex, pt 2

Seeing Ms. Moore bent over her desk was a fantastic sight. Her ass was magnificently shaped, like a heart, and her thighs were perfect. I took a brief moment to take it all in and then I was back in it, literally. I placed my hands on her hips and slid inside her wet pussy. I couldn't believe how tight she was! Even after that hammering I just gave her, she still managed to clench it on me. I was definitely dealing with a pro. I could hear her moans increase in volume and intensity with each thrust and it turned me on more and more. I wanted nothing else other than to please her in every possible way, and I was so glad that I was getting the chance. I could tell by the way she backed her ass up on me that she was enjoying all of this as much as I was and that she was determined to give as good as she got.

I reached forward, grabbing a fistful of hair in both hands and pulled, gently. "Pull harder," she screamed. I pulled harder. I had to push a silly image of a jockey riding a filly out of my mind, because that's exactly what it felt like, what with her ass bouncing against my thighs and my hands in her hair. I leaned back, my hands still pulling her hair, and looked down, getting even more turned on by the sight of her juices coating my dick as I cycled in and out of her. I let go of her hair and placed both hands on her thick ass, spreading her cheeks to give me an even better view. This was amazing.

"Spank me, David!" I could only do as requested. I was so surprised at this level of freakiness she was exhibiting. But then again, I guess a woman of her stature and in her position needed a strong release every now and again. I hoped this wasn't a onetime deal. I wanted to spank this ass for a long time coming, pun intended. I tapped her left cheek with my right hand, softly at first. "Harder!" Like I said earlier, all of this roughness was a little new for me, but I was willing to do anything to please Ms. Moore. I lifted my left hand high in the air and brought it down with a thunderous clap on her left ass cheek. "Oooh, yes!" So, that's how it is done, eh? I did it again, and then I switched to the right side. I loved the way her ass, firm and yet supple, jiggled with each smack. I was in paradise.

I could feel another nut coming, and I knew Ms. Moore wouldn't allow me to slow down, so I had to change positions. As much as I loved fucking her doggy-style, I had to switch it up or I wouldn't be good for much longer. I slipped out of her pussy and sat down on the chair behind me. She stood up, faced me and smiled. Without a word she came over to me and straddled my thighs, sliding my dick back inside her: pure paradise. Ms. Moore had plenty of experience under her theoretical belt, I could see. She started riding me like a pro. First she rode me flat, which caused her clit to rub against my pubic hair. I could tell she knew how to get herself off. She leaned forward, her breasts rubbing against my shirt and silk tie. I could feel her erect nipples through the fabric of my top as she continued to grind on me. I kissed her along the length of her neck, enjoying the smell of her perfume and the softness of her skin.

I knew she was racing for another orgasm when she started jumping on and off of my dick, causing pussy juice to fly all over our thighs. Her breasts were flying in my face and I was completely mesmerized. I reached around, grabbing her ample ass, and started moving with her, her pussy meeting every one of my thrusts with perfect timing. She rocked her head back and I knew she was about to explode.

"Daviiiid!" Now, if that didn't make me feel like a king, nothing would. She rocked her hips violently against me, her entire body thrashing with her powerful orgasm. I leaned into her and nibbled first on one nipple, then the next, becoming enchanted by how hard they were and how sweet her breasts tasted. She dug her nails into my back and I knew then what it was that she was into. She finally came down off of her sexual plateau. I wanted nothing more than to make her do it again.

She looked down at me lazily. "Mmmm...I didn't plan on this being in your job description, but if this is how you're going to fuck me, then I think I can make a permanent exception." I smiled, agreeing wholeheartedly.

"I like the sound of that, and I don't even want a raise." As she continued to sit in my lap I placed my arms under her thighs and instructed her to wrap her hands around my neck and to hold on. She looked at me quizzically. I winked, knowing that I was about to show her something new. I was also glad that I never neglected my time in the gym.

I stood up, her legs in the crease of my forearms and biceps, my hands maintaining a firm hold on her ass and her arms wrapped tightly around my neck. I was still inside her. When you're a young, horny man like me and you don't have sex for almost a year, porn becomes your best friend. You start to develop favorite "actors" and "actresses." Justin Slayer was my dude and I was about to do one of his signature moves.

"David, I know I'm too heavy for you to carry! What are you doing?!" I didn't respond. I was fit, I was healthy, and she was definitely NOT too heavy for me. I started to move myself in and out of her sweet canal while she was suspended in my arms, my balls swinging freely in the air. She knew she was in for a literal ride, so she hung on and started enjoying herself again. Once she realized that I could handle her weight and the situation, she even started moving with me, jumping up and down on my dick. Her pussy was so swollen around me and it was driving me crazy! I started fucking her harder and faster, just how I knew she wanted it and I could feel my balls slapping against the crack of her ass. I could feel her nectar spilling down my shaft. Her breasts were smashed against my chest as we clung to each other, as if for life.

I could feel her next orgasm approaching, as well as mine. "Cum with me, David!" I would be more than happy to oblige. Whatever the boss wants, right? I tightened my grip on her ass and began thrusting furiously, wanting to make this nut the best ever. I looked up to see her eyes rolling in the back of her head and sweat rolling down her face. Her pussy sucking on my dick let me know she was about to bust, too. I went in for the long stroke, making my balls slap that ass each time I threw myself into her. I felt my nuts swelling and I knew that we timed this one perfectly. She let out a howl and I growled into the air, both of us climaxing at the same time, our juices mixing into a lusty sex cocktail.

I sat her down on her desk because my energy was quickly draining out of me. She pulled me down to her, kissing me strong and deeply. I knew to enjoy this as much as I could, because tomorrow was back to business.

But for now, I enjoyed giving her the business. "I am so glad that you're the man for the job," she said with a wink.

Meet Me In The Shower

I follow you into the shower, admiring the way the water starts to wrap around your body. I can feel the steam in the air, taking pleasure in knowing that our love will soon be floating with it. I close the curtain behind us and face you, running my hands all over your wet frame. I look into your beautiful eyes and wonder: how can I be so lucky? This is going to be one shower not soon forgotten. I lean down and kiss your lips, darting my tongue in and out of your mouth as you do the same. Your passion is quickly building and I can feel the heat from your body meshing with the heat of the water.

I continue to kiss you, running my hands down your lithe body. I squeeze your ample ass, loving the weight, the feel, the silky smooth touch of each cheek in my hands. I pull your body closer to me, feeling your warmth in front of me and the heat from the shower head behind me. Your breasts are pressed tightly against my chest, your erect nipples tickling my ribs.

I lather you up with soap, enjoying the way it dances down your body as it races to the drain. I smile when I see the interesting and provocative ways it covers you before being washed away. I turn you around to face the rear of the shower so that I can admire your full and beautiful ass in its glory and wash your back. There's nothing wrong with a gentle soapy massage before sex, right?

You look back at me and wink, turning me on. You bend over the slightest amount, pushing your butt against my growing erection. I take my hand and slide it down your back until it reaches your honey pot. You're wet, but I know it's not from the water. I place both hands on your ass now, spreading you so that I can enter effortlessly. There is just the slightest bit of resistance as the water is firing across my right shoulder and falling down between you and I, pooling in the area that you and I touch. I lean forward to kiss your shoulders.

Your pussy takes me in. I love how tight you are. Your head goes back; a moan escapes from your lips. I push myself into you as deep as deep can be until my balls are hanging just above your clit. The water rushing across my back mixed in with the sensations of your tight pussy sucking on me are driving me wild. I pull out until just the head of my dick is inside you, only to slam it back in, your breath getting caught in your throat. I can feel the wetness of your juices all over my shaft as I continue in this fashion, in and out, in and out. I lean back, the stream of water rinsing all remnants of soap off of our bodies. I continue to thrust into you, my balls slapping against your clit, your breasts rocking back and forth.

You stand now, causing my dick to stand up inside you. You lean back, wrapping your arms around my neck and leaning your head back, giving me a chance to kiss, lick and suck on your neck. I love the way you feel, and the way you taste. I slow down my strokes, having to change my rhythm to match our position. I reach in front of you to massage your breasts. They're so nice, and more than a handful. Because there is water all over your body, your breasts are slippery to the touch. I play with your nipples, tweaking them. You moan and gasp in my ear. My dick gets harder still.

The water is beginning to lose some of its heat, so I turn the cold water down. I want to finish this with as much fire as we started with. Our bodies had cooled down a bit, so the sudden rise in temperature is a rush. You bend over again and give me The Look. I know you want to cum, and I want to cum with you. This time you are facing the shower head and the water is running down your back and splashing against my stomach and chest. I quicken my thrusts and match yours, driving you closer and closer to your impending orgasm. I can feel my balls swelling as your pussy tightens on me. That's the sign that you're about to explode. Your hands are on either side of the tub as you slam your ass into me, crying for that sweet release.

Finally, you get it. You freeze in place, the lips of your pussy locked onto me as your whole body seems to shut down. Your knees are locked as your nectar flows from your flower, sending me over the threshold. I start to cum inside you, our juices mixing into one delirium inducing cocktail. I hold onto your hips for balance as our moans echo throughout the bathroom. I can feel each spurt of cum flowing out of me and, it seems, each one is matched by a clenching of your labia.

We are spent. So is the hot water. You turn it all off as I reach for a towel. You turn and smile at me, a look of ultimate relaxation spread across your face. My soul agrees with that look. I've never felt so dirty while getting so clean.

The Ultimate Sex Story, pt 1.5

Diego…

We leave the pool hall amongst a sea of stares and giggles. I'm pretty sure that most, if not everyone, knows what happened. In fact, I think I saw someone putting away a camera phone as we were walking out. And the waitress didn't fully adjust her skirt before she walked back around the corner. Well, she'll have an interesting story to tell her friends later.

We get in my car, and I want to know what's our next stop on this tour of lust and debauchery. "My place," you tell me. Oh, yeah! You haven't 'broken it in' yet, right? Your place it is, then.

As we drive down Broad Street, we're laughing about the experience we just enjoyed. That was definitely unusual. I've done it in public places before, but never where getting caught was so close and actually invited! What a rush! Apparently, you are still excited about the way the evening has been going because no sooner do we pass The Boulevard heading east than your hand starts to tickle my thigh. Wait, no...that's not my thigh.

My desire is still hard and strong given the excitement of the evening and in one swift move, you manage to free me of the restraints of my shorts. Damn! Without a second thought, you are going down on me, moistening the tip of my dick with your tongue.

I pull up to a red light and adjust myself so that you can pull my shorts down to get better access to my stiffness without hindering my driving ability. Thankfully, for once, this is a long light and I lean my head back for a moment enjoying the beautiful things you are doing to me with your mouth. I rub the back of your head, not coaxing you, but loving the skills that you have. I open my eyes to check on the status of the signal: still red; good.

I hear something to my left and look out the window to see a huge mud covered 4X4 with two rednecks leaning out of the passenger window and on the verge of falling onto their faces in the middle of the street. I roll down the window.

"Damn! That looks good right there! She doin' work, ain't she?!" Ha...fuckin' rednecks.

"Yes, sir, she is. Damn good wo...oh, shit!" I lose focus momentarily because you really ARE doing good work. The light turns green. Whew!

We finally make it to your apartment, and I enjoyed every beautiful minute of the ride. But now it's time for another sort of ride. Thankfully, it is dark outside when we park because I absolutely refuse to pull my shorts up all the way. What's even funnier is you leading me to the elevator...by my cock. As we load the elevator, you're caught off guard by me slamming you with just enough force against the wall and tonguing you down. Your breasts overflow my palms as I slide my hands under your bra and play with your already erect nipples.

We make it to your floor and stumble out of the elevator, you still clutching my dick and me kissing all over your neck. We're like two extremely horny teenagers ducking class.

As we clumsily make our way to the end of the hall towards your door, we hear an all too familiar noise. What was that? Remembering where we are, we let each other go for the moment and try to focus. There it is again! Oh, hell! That was a moan if I've ever heard one. And it's coming from your neighbors. Well, they're a couple doors down and across the hall, but there is some serious messin' around going on. No, wait: that's something pounding against the wall. Yeah, that's fucking!

"I wonder who can be louder: us or them?" I ask you as I tweak your right nipple. As if in response, you grab my hand and damn near drag my ass towards your door, barely getting the key in the lock.

We're scarcely in the door and we're already all over each other. "Fuck the foreplay. Fuck ME!" you groan in my ear. No problem. Within moments, we are both completely naked. I pick you up with no effort and slide your already dripping wet pussy onto my dick, with you emitting a moan so guttural in my ear that I feel myself getting even harder. I squeeze your ass, feeling the juice from your pussy sliding down over my fingers. This whole experience is turning me on even more.

Your legs are wrapped around my waist and your arms are gripping my neck, as if you're hanging on for dear life. Although I am standing, I push your back against the nearest wall and commence to fucking the shit out of you. I can feel the juice from your pussy slapping against my thighs, your cries of ecstasy echoing in my ears. Harder, you tell me. Faster, you scream. Each and every plateau that you reach yanks me along with you. The feeling is fantastic.

I lean back and watch your titties bounce up and down as my dick slides in and out of you repeatedly, covered in your slick and sexy sauce. "Put me down; I want you behind me!"

We damn near run over to your couch and you kneel on it, looking behind at me with a look of pure lust. Damn. I enter you so easily and feel your body shudder with excitement. I start slowly, just to make sure that I don't hurt you. Although I want this to last, you and I both know that we will be cumming multiple times tonight.

"Fuck meeee!" you scream as the couch starts to pound into the wall. I hope your neighbors are sound sleepers or, better yet, out of town for the evening. I slap your ass with just enough force to drive you insane with passion but not hard enough to leave a mark.

We're like this, two rabbits fucking, with juices everywhere, when I finally get ready to come to a climax. As is your style, you wait until that first drop threatens to explode from the head of my penis, and you pull me out and turn around faster than lightning. Oh no, not this! You take me into your mouth before I can start to run away, grabbing my ass with your hands and pulling me further and further into your warm mouth as I continue to spill my cum into you. It takes every ounce of strength I have to not pass out or convulse onto the floor. This orgasm is too much, but you won't let go!

Finally you have drained the last out of me. I know there was a moment there when I was probably screaming like a bitch. We're lying in the middle of the floor laughing, sweating profusely, when there begins a knocking at the door. Who the hell could that be?

The Ultimate Sex Story, pt 2

Michelle…

I scramble to the door wondering who it could be. I look out of the peep hole and am staring at what I believe to be the back of a man's head. Instead of putting on clothes, I slightly crack open the door and peek my head around it to inquire who was there. I see one of my guy neighbors from the other side of the elevator. He's saying something about using my phone; however I am not quite listening to him because I am staring at his shirtless body. I tell him to hang on while I grab my phone.

I find the phone amongst the clothes we ripped off our bodies during our steamy, wild romp and grab a coat to throw on to give my neighbor the phone. In my usual fashion I ask you to stay out of sight because I don't want my neighbors to think I am some wild sort of freak. Because there was a man at the door, you happily oblige to my request until I re-open the door. Apparently I missed the fact that my neighbor's girlfriend needed the phone. She is standing there, wearing running shorts and a wife beater. It is apparent by her extremely erect nipples that she is not wearing a bra. She gives me the once over, realizing that under my coat I am naked and gives her boyfriend a sultry grin.

As she begins to speak, you get up off of your resting place on the floor and begin to walk to the door. The girl in front of me begins to stammer through her phone conversation and as I follow her gaze I turn around to find you right behind me stroking your dick, giving this woman at my door one of your "come hither" looks. Before I can react you pin me up against the door jamb and begin to untie the belt on my coat while attacking my neck. We are halfway in the hallway and halfway in the apartment. The guy, who had been standing out of sight, hears the commotion and comes into view. The two of them are in shock, however they haven't moved. As you take my coat off to reveal my naked body you begin kissing me while maintaining eye contact with the girl. I kneel down to start giving you head, all the time never taking my eyes off of our audience.

Another moment goes by before the guy walks up behind his girl and begins to lift up her shirt, showing off her beautiful plump breasts, and her unusually erect, but extremely beautiful pink nipples. He begins caressing them and while we have stopped to check them out I take her hand and place it on your dick. She begins to stroke your dick, while you suck on her left breast. I join you and begin to suck on her right breast while her man reaches down and begins to rub my clit.

A door in the background slams, snapping us back into the reality that we are standing in the hallway. I lead everyone into the living room and move the small coffee table out of the floor. I turn around to see you standing in the middle of the floor, looking up to the ceiling in ecstasy from her on her knees going down on you. She is taking all of you into her mouth. I see her man, who has taken this opportunity to take his clothes off, and I walk over to him and start to stroke his dick. He stops me immediately and walks me over to his girlfriend. He gets her attention so that I can position myself for her to sit on my face. I immediately begin to taste her sweetness and realize that she gets almost as wet as I do. Her man begins to eat me out, which makes me quiver, sending up a chain reaction to the girl, who in turn sends that sensation to you.

You begin to moan just a little, which excites the hell out of me. I begin really taking it to this chick's clit while sliding a finger in her tight ass. The pleasure she feels makes her quiver, which in turn gives you a gentle tightening sensation on your dick. This chain reaction continues for a while, until the head she is giving you feels so good your legs tremble just a little.

Her man sits on the couch, and tells us to do our thing. His girlfriend doesn't even flinch. She immediately turns around on my face to move into a sixty-nine. Seeing her sexy heart-shaped ass bent over my face, you instantly kneel down to lick it... you just can't help yourself! You start licking her ass while I am licking her clit and we both are getting off on the fact that we are making this chick squeal. She tries to run from us and we both laugh and hold her down, torturing her even more with our tongues, giving her a violent orgasm.

I stop long enough to tell you to "fuck her". You enter her pussy from behind while she is still bent over my face. As you enter her you feel my tongue licking your balls and as you exit her she feels my tongue on her clit. You then realize how wet she is and begin to fuck her with a little more force. I move from up under her, and make my way over to her boyfriend who has been jacking off to the live porno unfolding in front of him. I attempt to give him head, but he insists on only eating my pussy and watching us. Of course I take him up on the offer and lay back on the couch, feeling his tongue caressing my pussy, watching you and his girl fuck.

You look over realizing you have an audience and begin to fuck her more forcefully. The harder you fuck her, the tighter her pussy gets around your dick. This excites her man, who decides he no longer only wants to eat me. He immediately flips me over and enters my pussy from behind. The two of you begin to compete to see who can make the girl they are fucking scream the loudest. All you can hear is the forceful sound of pelvises thrusting against ass. Her boyfriend picks me up and sits me on the kitchen counter, places my legs on his shoulders and is violently fucking the hell out of me.

Though I am screaming my head off in ecstasy we manage to make and keep eye contact with each other. I give you a look that clearly tells you that I want to feel you inside of me again. At that very moment, the chick calls out to her man and tells him she wants to sit on his face. We re-arrange ourselves and I lay down on the floor, spreading my legs for you to enter me - missionary style. As you start to enter my extremely tight, super-soaked pussy, you feel a hand on your backside. You look over your shoulder and see the chick sitting on her man's face fascinated with your behind. As you turn back around to me you begin to feel her tongue on your left cheek, and her hand massaging your right. Then in an instant you feel her tongue begin to slide down the middle of your cheeks. You shudder in pleasure as there is yet another knock at the door. Who could it be this time...?

Give Thanks

Thanksgiving was never my favorite holiday. I almost always had to work. I was usually single and my family consisted of my terrier, Bowser. All of that meant that I was alone for the holidays and Thanksgiving just brought the season in with a dismal bang. I would usually head to a local soup kitchen, do some volunteer work. Then I'd head home to watch the end of the Cowboys or Lions game and fall asleep with Bowser in my lap, a half finished six pack of Bud Light by my side. At least this way I was able to make someone feel better about their day, even though mine was sure to end in drunken depression.

I was sure this year would be no different. I volunteered every year at the Heaven's Blessing Center on Main Street just to get out, get some air and feel like my life wasn't a complete waste. Don't misunderstand: I'm not really depressed. I'm just bored. I've been single for years and haven't gotten laid in about that long. I tried the dating scene and it just wasn't for me. So I decided that the right woman would fall in my lap when the time was right. Apparently the gods have a broken watch because the time hasn't been right yet. I'm not complaining though. I enjoy my simple life.

I walked the mile that it took me to get to Heaven's Blessing, the wind causing me to pull up the collar on my peat coat. It was cloudy, windy, and every business on the street was closed or closing early.

sigh

Could this day get any gloomier? Traffic was light, which was always a good thing for this city. I didn't have to worry about bumping into a million people while I walked. And, thankfully, what would have normally been a 40 minute walk was accomplished in about 20 minutes. What a difference traffic makes.

I walked into Heaven's Blessing expecting a decent crowd as usual, but it was packed! I heard someone yell my name as I hung my coat in the volunteer's closet. I looked in the direction from whence it came and was surprised to see an angel. Actually, she was another volunteer named Angel. I only saw her once a year, which was no surprise for a city this size. What was a surprise, however, was the fact that she remembered my name.

I walked over to her and as we gave that customary "hey, how you doin'/how you been/well, that's good" greeting/hug she alerted me to our situation: more homeless to feed, less volunteers to help. I rolled up my sleeves and dug in where I could. I looked out on the sea of hungry faces and was thankful for being able to help. Occasionally, I would look over at Angel to make sure she was handling things with the dressings. She worked efficiently and like a pro, was doing a much better job than I was with carving the turkeys. At one point she caught me looking at her and something strange happened. Actually, it was a feeling that was foreign to me. Angel and I never talked much while here at Heaven's Blessing but we knew a little about each other. One thing I didn't know, though, was whether she was married or not. She never wore a ring but I assumed that was because she didn't want to get it dirty. She always came alone, but that could be because her significant other wasn't into volunteering.

She caught me looking at her and apparently I'd been staring. She asked me if I was alright and I nodded yes, embarrassed. The line had died down and everyone was eating their food so we had a while before anyone came up for seconds. The other volunteers fixed themselves plates at this time and everyone just sat and talked usually. I wasn't hungry, though, at least not for turkey. I don't know what stirred within me but I walked up to Angel, feeling bold and confident, completely out of the ordinary for me.

"Where's your boyfriend this year?" I don't know what was wrong with me! I'd never ask someone a question like that, and so bold and blatantly. Angel didn't seem offended or put off in the least, though.

"I don't have a boyfriend. No husband." She waved her ring finger at me. "Just me and my cat." I looked at her face and seemed to notice for the first time just how beautiful she was. Her skin looked so smooth and fair; her hair was tied up in a bun but I could just imagine it cascading down her back. I could tell it was long. She had a cute Carolina blue sweater, which fit her frame perfectly. Her breasts were perky and filled the sweater nicely. She was very shapely and filled her jeans in a manner that you only see on T.V. Why hadn't I noticed her before? "Are you ok?" she asked, interrupting my thoughts. Shit, I'd been staring again!

"Yes! I'm so sorry. It's just that, I was wondering…umm…" So much for that sudden boost of confidence I'd had earlier. "I was wondering how could someone such as you be single?"

"Such as me?" She laughed. "I've been single for a while now," she explained. "Work, gym, home…that's my life." I co-signed on her sentiment. We grabbed a cup of hot apple cider apiece and walked into the back. We discussed our lives, our jobs, our pets, seemingly everything.

After we were through with the serving and volunteering for the day, Angel shocked me and asked if I wanted to come to her place. Like the intelligent man I usually am, I accepted the invite. She lived two miles in the other direction, but thankfully the wind had died down, so we continued our conversation in relative peace: no weather, no traffic, and no annoyances.

By the time we reached her apartment, I felt as if I'd known her for years. She gave me a brief tour and poured us some drinks. I don't normally drink, but that Amoretto smelled divine. It tasted even better. After about another hour of talking and drinking, I was feeling fun and fancy free. We were both on her loveseat comparing stories of loves lost and hearts broken and I just threw myself at her. I don't know what has possessed me today, but I liked it. I leaned into her and kissed her square on the lips. I pulled away, again embarrassed at my actions. I couldn't read the look on her face. Shock? Anger? She leaned forward. I thought she was going to stand and tell me to leave. Instead, she returned the kiss, pushing me onto my back.

Her kiss was so warm and yet sweet. Her tongue found its way into my mouth and danced with mine, igniting a fire within me that hadn't existed in so long. I wanted to feel this forever, but a sudden burning came from another part of me, and I knew then that I had to have her in another way as well. Angel must have felt the same heat because she started to pull my shirt out of my jeans and over my head, kissing my stomach and chest as she did so. Thank goodness I worked out and I had a decent looking six pack for her to kiss on. After getting my shirt off, she leaned back and lifted her sweater over her head. I saw it all in slow motion and it was beautiful. She had on a white lace bra underneath that held her breasts up as if in solemn offering. Without thinking, I reached up and grabbed a set of breasts for the first time in half a decade. They were firm, round and perfect. And just like that, my pants became entirely too tight. As she was sitting on my lap, Angel must have felt my erection. She got from on top of me and unzipped my pants. That had to have been the fastest I'd ever taken my pants off. She laughed at my eagerness and slid out of her pants, revealing her matching panty set. I whimpered.

She allowed me to drink in her body as she took of her bra and panties. Wow, she even shaved 'down there!' I was impressed, and in heaven. I remembered that I hadn't eaten anything earlier, so it was time for me to make up for that. She stood in front of me while I sat up on the loveseat, lifting her left leg and placing it beside me. I slid down and kissed her juicy slit, admiring the sexy fragrance it emitted. She tasted just as lovely as she looked. She grabbed the back of my head, grinding me into her, so I know I must have been doing something right. I ran my tongue up and down her wet pussy lips, occasionally probing into her and sucking on her labia. I could feel her moans coursing through her body and every time she shuddered, it caused my nose to touch her clit ever so lightly.

It has been such a long time since I've seen a pussy, let alone eaten one, that I didn't want it to end. I was in paradise. I played with her some more, fingering her with my middle finger while licking and sucking on her clit. I could feel Angel getting wetter and wetter until she finally exploded amidst a rain of cum and ecstasy. I loved watching her ride the wave of her orgasm as her knees buckled beneath her.

I guided her to sit down on my lap, my hardness sliding into her effortlessly with the assistance of her amazingly wet pussy. She fit onto me like a new glove: so tight, and yet the perfect fit. My head rocked back with the sensation of being inside her. I saw yellow suns, purple moons, and green balloons! It had been so long since I'd gotten any, and it was a bonus that when I DO get some, it feels like this. I pulled her farther onto my shaft, wanting to fill her up as much as possible. Angel started moving her hips, riding me and sending me flying. I pulled her body closer to mine to feel her warmth and to lick and suck on her luscious breasts. Her nipples were already hard and I could feel them getting harder in my mouth. Despite the heat each of our bodies was emanating, I could feel the goose bumps on her skin.

She continued to ride me, her arms on my shoulders and her head thrown back, our moans filling the air. She leaned down and kissed me, hard. I wasn't used to it, but I liked it. Based on our conversation, I knew that it had been a long time since she had been with a man and was taking advantage of it just like I was. I couldn't blame her. Our tongues danced with each other, enjoying the last of the Amoretto liqueur we'd had earlier.

She lifted herself off of me, to my dismay, and gave me a look, one I'd never seen before. Her eyes looked to be filled with crazed lust. It turned me on even more. She took my hand, helping to stand. She let go and started walking away, towards where I learned her bedroom was during the tour. She spoke over her shoulder as I watched her sexy and shapely ass walk away from me, "I want you to fuck me from behind…you up for it?" I raced her to her bedroom.

She jumped onto her bed, her ass facing me. I was delirious. This was turning out to be a helluva day. I kneeled behind her, taking a moment to run my hands over her behind, loving how soft and smooth she kept her skin. Damn, I was in love with her booty. I laughed to myself at the thought.

"Fuck me, please," she pleaded. She wouldn't have to ask twice. My dick, still hard as a rock, entered her from behind effortlessly. She used her Kegel muscles to pull me deeper into her. I gasped at the unfamiliar sensation and then went for broke. I grabbed each cheek with a hand and started pounding my dick into her. Her cries and moans bounced off the walls as I commenced to attacking that pussy with everything I could muster. I'd never been accused of being the greatest lover, but I sure as hell was going to give it my all that night! The sight of her pussy sucking on me drove me wild. I loved it. Her ass was shaking with each thrust and her moans were rocking the walls. I could feel myself racing to my orgasm. Her pussy got tighter as she rushed towards hers as well. I leaned forward, wrapping my arms around her and squeezing her swaying breasts. She turned her head towards me and kissed me on the mouth, she sucking on my tongue as I pumped furiously within her.

I was so close to orgasm, and I wanted to prolong it, but I had a feeling that this wasn't going to be the only round tonight. I worked furiously, wanting to feel cum spouting from the tip of my dick. My balls were slapping against her clit, heightening her orgasms. I pulled out right before I erupted, showering her back with my seed. I moaned aloud, unable to control my mouth or my body. I fell backwards onto her bed, spent.

Angel turned around with a grin. "It seems like I have a quite a few orgasms to be thankful for today. And now, I must return the favor." She leaned over, kissing the tip of my penis, which instantly began to get hard again. Indeed, I am VERY thankful this year.

The Ultimate Sex Story, pt 3

Diego…

"WHO IS IT?!?!" we all scream at the same time. This is some serious shit going on right now and the last thing we need or want is to be disturbed. I'm thinking to myself, "If this is a nosy ass neighbor or bill collector or ANYONE who ain't gonna' add to this party, then they can kick rocks!"

I'm not getting up to answer the door since I am hilt deep in your pussy. You're not getting up because I won't let you. Your male neighbor can't get up because he has juice running down his face. That leaves her. I'll call her Jane and him we'll name John.

Jane gets up, still butt ass naked and yanks open the door. "Either you fuckin', suckin', or gettin' the hell on!" Wow, she doesn't like to be interrupted. I start laughing because this isn't her apartment and she doesn't know who the caller could be. I hear someone on the other side of the door stammering, more than likely from surprise at the very naked Jane at the door with a look of venom on her face.

"Uh...I, uh...umm...have a, uh...a, um...pizza?" We didn't order pizza and I call this fact out to him while I slowly continue my strokes into you. John has also moved and is currently feeding his dick to you as you lay on your back. "Uh...yeah...um...I know...your neighbors, uh...the people next door did."

I ask him if it is policy to deliver the pizza to the next door neighbors if the customer isn't home and to stop stuttering because it's annoying me and ruining my focus. The bass in my voice seemed to make him man up. "Actually, bruh, I thought I heard some fuckin', man. I can't lie."

Bruh?

Jane pulls him inside and the three of us get a really good look at him. I stop what I'm doing because you've started to sit up. You look hungry, and something tells me it isn't for pizza. Jane takes the pizza from him, she seems a tad ghetto, and comments about how cold it is and asks how long he'd been outside the door listening.

"Um...a-about," he starts.

"Stop stuttering, please," I implore.

"Ten to fifteen minutes."

You jump in surprise and with Jane's assistance, back him against the door. What happens next can only be described at the funniest thing I'd seen in a long time. The two of you throw a verbal barrage of questions and accusations at the poor young man until his knees go weak. Poor thing. He looks like he'd have more spine. He's young, black and about 6 feet with a couple inches. Maybe 6'3"? He's thin, but not what I would call "skinny." He smells good, too, but I think that is my stomach talking and the fact that we haven't eaten since we started this festival of fucking earlier in the evening. He's got a nice, recent fade going on and two earrings, one for each ear. His facial features are strong, too.

After about five minutes of getting cussed out by two very sexy, very naked women, his features fall and he mumbles an apology.

"Oh, hell no!" Jane continues on him. "You gotta' pay that for that bullshit, cuz that is just rude. I have just the idea." He offers to give us the pizza and be on his way, but before he can open the door and be on his way you and Jane push and pull him towards the center of the room and sit on the couch. You spread your legs and Jane does likewise. I look at John and smile. I know exactly where this is going. Poor guy is about to get the best tip of his life.

One word. "Eat."

Apparently, that shy persona of his is just a facade, because no sooner do the words escape your mouth than he is on his knees and going for broke! He switches it up between your pussy and Jane's as if he was a DJ in the club on the turntables. John and I exchange looks of impression. First, he is on your pussy, licking and lapping while fingering Jane and then he switches it up. He begins to suck the juice out of Jane's pussy while rubbing and gently squeezing on your clit. Geez, this boy is good!

Moans and groans emit from your mouth, further fueling young Pizza Boy's desire. I can see it in his actions. He plans to eat well tonight.

You know, this is great and all, but John and I are feeling a little left out. Wait, no, just me. John is beside me, albeit not too closely, and jacking his dick for all he is worth. I can tell he really likes watching his girl get hers. Well, that only works for me to a certain extent. I climb up on the couch and place myself right in front of you, clearing my throat as I do so. You open your eyes, and seeing my massive erection in front of you, flash me the most beautiful smile. Cute. Too bad it will be full of dick in a minute. I feel Jane massaging my balls. Her neat and manicured nails feel so good rubbing against my nuts that I can't help but to tilt my head back and moan.

Not to be outdone, you take as much of me into your mouth as you can. Damn, this is the life. The double rush of her licking and sucking on my balls combined with your warm mouth along my shaft nearly sends me over the edge. I figure that standing up on the couch isn't the best place to have an orgasm. I step down just as Pizza Boy gets up, wiping his mouth and face at the same time. Yeah, he doesn't seem so shy anymore.

"Let that be a lesson to you," Jane says with a wink. "No peeping Toms." He smiles at this and comments that he has to get back to work, but enjoyed the time.

After he leaves, the four of us look at each other with hard dicks and erect nipples. Where were we?

The Ultimate Sex Story, pt 4

Michelle…

Since the pizza boy gave into Jane and I, my pussy is literally dripping with wetness, which makes me hungry for some more of your dick. I make my way over to you and tell you to hit it from the back. As we get into position, Jane and John sit down on the couch to take what I thought was a breather. I could not be anymore wrong. Jane really shows her dominant side by ordering us to fuck the way she wants us to.

We give each other a "what the fuck?!" look but being the sexually curious people we are we more than welcome playing the role of puppets in the Jane Sex Show. Jane's first instruction was for you to lick my ass. (Jane is my kind of girl) I bend over, while standing, in front of you and you kneel behind me and begin to lick. Jane keeps on telling you to make my ass real wet. You glance over at Jane and John and see them both masturbating and that they are so into watching us that they are about to fall off the couch. After a few minutes Jane tells us what she really wants us to do.

She orders you to enter me from behind. No wait, I didn't hear her correctly. She wants you to enter me IN the behind. She orders me down on my knees, "Head down, ass up!" You begin to enter my tight asshole. I quiver from the pleasurable pain of feeling my ass stretch to accommodate you. You work it in about halfway before Jane jumps up off the couch and joins us on the floor. She is facing you with one hand on each of my ass cheeks and is spreading them apart for you to have better access. At this point my moans have gone back and forth from pleasure and pain, but I do not tell you to stop. Maybe I was scared of what Jane might do if I did.

Once you work your entire dick in my asshole Jane goes on a spanking frenzy. She is literally tuning my ass red while ordering you to continue pumping my ass with your dick. "Harder! Deeper! Faster! Fuck that bitch!" My ass begins to clench around your dick as I begin to come. As your balls are bouncing off my pussy you realize they are completely covered in my juices. Then, almost out of nowhere you feel an orgasm coming on. Jane orders you to shoot your load into her mouth, porno style. "Gimme' that money shot, baby!"

You cum harder than you ever have and nut goes everywhere, on my ass, in her mouth, on her hair, in her eye. Definitely a money shot. You collapse from exhaustion, as do I, but realize your dick is still hard and you want some more...

The Ultimate Sex Story, pt 5 (FINALE)

Diego…

I see now that John is the submissive one in the relationship. I really want him to get in on the fun, and now may be the time to do that. "John, come here, man." He steps over, a little tentatively, and stands beside Jane, who is still licking my seed from her fingers. "Lay down," I instruct him. He does so with no hesitation, and on his stomach. Eh? Ok, I can work around that. "Jane, commence to licking John's ass like he was a bowl of ice cream and it is 90 degrees outside." She starts running her tongue up and down his cheeks and down the crack of his ass with relish. I can visibly see John's body shudder with excitement and pleasure. Good.

Once she gets into a good rhythm, you become mesmerized by the sight of her very soft and shapely ass wiggling in front of you. It looks as if it is just begging for attention. You crawl over to her and bury your face in her fat pussy from behind. She squeals with surprise and then pushes herself back onto you. While she is still licking John all over his ass, she reaches around, grabs both of her juicy ass cheeks, and spreads herself so that you have more access to her honey pot.

I am so turned on by the licking' train in front of me and I don't know what to do. Do I get down on my knees and bury my tongue in your ass again, or do I shove eight inches of dick in you? How about one and then the other?

Just as I am about to get down on my knees and join the party, John turns over and grabs the back of Jane's head, sliding her mouth onto his cock. Hmm, submissive no longer, it seems. I can tell she wants to ride his dick because she is really starting to push her pussy back onto your face. She wants penetration and she wants it now. I grab your hair and pull you back from her, gently enough to not hurt but hard enough to please. As soon as you take your face away, she slides John's dick out of her mouth with a *pop* and jumps on his dick. I can hear the saliva that coats his dick rubbing against the saliva and juices from her pussy, and it sounds good. She straddles him, placing both of her legs on either side of his body, and leans forward, kissing him passionately.

I nudge you forward towards her ass that is still moving softly and slowly up and down on John's stiff dick. You start to lick at her asshole and down the length of John's cock all the way to his balls, which are dripping with Jane's juice. I'd describe the speed that they are at as "love-making." They're moving nice and slow, enjoying the atmosphere and giving you ample time to lick and suck on everything you want to.

As you get into a nice rhythm- you nibble on Jane's ass as she is moving her pussy up on his shaft, prodding her asshole with your tongue at the height of her ride, licking the base of his dick as she slides down, and sucking on his balls as she gets all of him in her- I move behind you and start to rub on your ass. You jump the slightest bit; I know your ass still stings from that hellacious and yet gratifying beating that Jane gave you. I commence to kissing your left cheek while gently rubbing and massaging your right one and then switch it up.

The four of us have slowed things down a bit and it feels nice. Luxurious moans fill the air. Jane has sat up a little to give John access to her bountiful breasts; he is sucking, licking, and loving them. I move my face in between your ass cheeks and stick my hot, wet tongue out as far as possible and slide it in your asshole with ease. I hear you moan in front of me and your ass clenches, as if wanting me to stay there forever. I continue to rub on your ass while sliding my tongue in and out of you as far as possible. I mix that up with sliding my tongue up and down the crack of your ass, getting everything nice, juicy and extremely wet.

Eventually, I feel as if I can't take any more. My dick is literally aching to slide inside you. I sit up and admire for a second the sight of your face still buried in Jane's ass and her pussy sliding up and down on his pole. I place my hands on the small of your back and press the very tip of my dick against your wetness. Normally, I would tease the hell out of you until you begged for me to fuck you. But this is not the time for that. I push myself against your pussy hole and feel only the slightest resistance from your tight pussy as I enter you. I grab a hold of your hips and push myself in you until my balls are kissing your clitoris. I stop for a moment, enjoying the heat coming from you and the way your pussy is vibrating against my dick. I slowly slide back out, admiring the even lines of juice that your pussy is spreading along the length of me.

Needless to say, your attention is no longer on sucking and licking John and Jane. I notice that they're in their own little world right now and that world no longer has a slow speed. She is bouncing up and down on his dick as if she is trying to impale herself with it. His knees are brought up behind her, making sure she doesn't fall over backwards. Her titties are flying in the air and so is her hair. His eyes are focused intently on her and her pleasure, or maybe they're following her breasts as they jump in front of him. Her head is tilted back and her eyes are seemingly glued shut. Her mouth, however, is wide open and she is screaming in absolute ecstasy. I think that was an orgasm.

Not to be outdone, I start to increase the tempo of my thrusts in and out of you. With each stroke, I turn it up a notch. Before long, you are pushing your ass back onto me as if you too are trying to feel my dick in the top of your stomach. I use one hand to slap you on the ass and the other, my right one, to reach out and grab your hair. Now all that can be heard is the sound of my balls slapping against your clit followed by intermittent slaps against your ass at my left hand along with Jane's screams throughout the apartment.

I look down and smile at the sight of your ass straining back against me and the way your ass jiggles when it hits me. I also see the way your asshole winks at me. I stick one of my fingers in my mouth, getting it nice and wet for what I am about to do now.

I slow down just enough to work my wet middle finger in your asshole and then pick the pace back up. This seems to drive you over, because I instantly feel your pussy getting wetter and wetter. You're building up to an orgasm and you start bucking your back. Oh yeah, this is going to be good! I use my right arm to hold your back down while pumping furiously in and out of your pussy and fingering your asshole.

I hear Jane getting louder and louder in the background. I look over at them just as she starts to convulse on John's dick. Oh, she's one of 'those types' of cummers, huh? As her body shaking starts to calm down, you get louder and louder as a climax rocks your body. I continue thrusting in and out of you as your pussy throws more and more of your juices onto my stomach, my thighs, and my dick.

Once you finally come down from your plateau, I feel my balls starting to swell and my dick getting harder than before. I don't think I can hold on much longer. Apparently John is in the same position. "Cum baby, CUM!" the two of you scream at us. I get a few more strokes in until I am on the verge of exploding inside of you. John and I pull out at the same time and I have barely enough time to direct Jane to your side as John and I let loose with hot streams of cum on the two of you. This is the most powerful orgasm I have had in a very long time. I continue stroking my dick as more and more of my seed spills out of me. The two of you are directly in front of us catching every drop that you can and helping us come to completion by rubbing and sucking on our balls. Oh, my damn!

When John and I are finally spent, I collapse on the couch, out of breath and of cum. I enjoy the sight in front of me of you and Jane cleaning one another by licking all over the other's body. Damn, that is a sexy sight. Full of masculine pride, John and I look at each other and give up daps...

Passion, pt 1

Their passion was so great, so intense. He wanted so badly to steal her spirit and consume her love and her lust. She wanted nothing more than to give every fiber of her being to him. Not three moments after him entering her house did the flames of passion ignite within them both and they were all over each other. Their kisses, strong and fierce, were long and combined with their hands running courses all over each other's bodies. He took a moment, just one moment, to break that kiss and gaze upon her body. Her frame, petite and sensual, was a physical melody to his eyes. Everything about her screamed love, beauty, attraction. He was in love at the first sight of her, every time he saw her.

She took that brief moment to grab his hand, pulling him behind her as she led him into her bedroom. As they nearly ran into her bedchamber, he gazed at her sexiness from behind and admired her tight, soft ass beneath that black negligee. Her shoulders were exposed and he could imagine his tongue and lips caressing her them. Her hair ran past her shoulders and he couldn't wait to feel it through his fingers. Once they entered the bedroom, she turned to face him, again kissing him with the kisses of her mouth,

He wanted to take his time and prolong the experience, but his loins were impatient this evening. That was a fitting emotion, because her lust was also screaming for release. They kissed each other passionately as they both fumbled with his clothes, nearly ripping his shirt and pants off. Finally he was down to nothing but his boxers. She gazed upon his physique, clearly impressed with this fine specimen of man that she was about to devour. She leaned against the edge of her bed as he stepped to her, lifting her lingerie above her head and shoulders, admiring the way the glow from the moon outside the window accented her lovely breasts. He sighed deeply as he leaned forward to take one nipple into his mouth. She gasped as the warmth from his mouth engulfed her breasts and sent shudders through her body. It had been so long, too long, since she had felt a man's touch.

While still sucking on her delicious and beautiful breasts, he grabbed her waist, lifting her onto the bed. She back crawled away from him, but not without a pout: she didn't want him to stop pleasing her chest, but instead to join her on the bed. He knew what she desired and crawled on the bed with her as she laid back, her hands playing with her own nipples. He kissed her ankles. Then he started kissing up her legs and thighs: first the left, then the right leg, then the left one again, all the while admiring how amazingly soft and smooth her legs were. Finally, he arrived at her honey pot. She sighed, knowing what was in store. It took only the slightest nudge from his chin to get her to spread her legs, inviting him to her. He inhaled her essence, loving how sweet she smelled, desiring to taste her.

She continued to play with her breasts, kneading and rubbing her mounds as he commenced to licking her pussy, sucking ever so lightly on her clit. Her moans were low in volume as he teased her privacy, enjoying the feeling of her wetness against his nose and mouth. She wanted more and her legs wrapped around his head and neck let him know so. The time for games was over. He placed his arms under her legs, clamping down on her thighs so that she couldn't run away and began to attack her pussy in earnest. Her juices were all over his face now as he feasted on her sweetness. Her moans were no longer low, but higher in volume and intensity, much like her impending orgasm. The pleasure was too much! She tried to crawl away, but he wasn't having it. He locked his arms even tighter around her, rowing his tongue between her clit and her pussy lips, swallowing every ounce of juice she threw at him. She was stuck: she couldn't take the amount of pleasure he was giving her, but she didn't want it to end.

Her hands ran lines between pulling on her breasts and grabbing and massaging his scalp between her legs. It was divine. She knew she was about to cum and this was the most powerful one she'd ever felt...OOH! Her hips buckled against him and her body began to convulse involuntarily. Using both hands, she grabbed his head, forcing him to suck every drop of cum out of her pussy. The force wasn't necessary, however: that was exactly what he planned on doing. He continued to lick, kiss, and suck on her until she had given him everything that she possibly could. Eventually her body relaxed, her thighs sore from clamping around his head and shoulders. She breathed a long, deep sigh of content, adrenaline and passion coursing through her veins. She looked up at him with lust in her eyes. He wore her out from the cunnilingus, but she wanted more. She looked down in the direction of his boxers and then back at his eyes. He got the hint. Kicking off his underwear, he stood before her with his erection steadily growing. She smiled with lustful anticipation. She had never seen one so large. She couldn't wait for him to fill and satisfy her every desire.

Passion, pt 2

A million things were rushing through her head at this moment. Should she pounce on him like the ravenous lioness that she was? Should she be docile and let him have his way with her? Or should she offer up resistance, toying with his manhood and emotions and make him fight for it? She didn't have long to debate with her options, because he was already on top of her, sucking on her neck while his erection probed eagerly at the entrance to her sweetness. Her pussy was slick with her juices and desire, allowing him to slide into her tightness with relative ease. He could feel the pressure from her surrounding walls and didn't want to hurt her, but at the same time he wanted to fill her with every inch of his being.

She gasped with delightful pleasure as he opened her up more and more with each passing moment. She opened her eyes to look into his, hers pleading to be ravished in every way possible. His presence was so dominating but caring at the same time. She could tell that he wanted nothing more than to please her, and the slight pain she felt at being stretched open by his girth was a very welcome feeling. She tried to open herself to him even more by wrapping her legs around his back, pushing her hips against his, wanting him to dive deeper than anyone ever had. He was well on his way to accomplishing that feat.

He had to take his time. It had been a while since he had gotten any, and even longer since he felt pussy this sweet, tight and divine. Each stroke teased the both of them. He would slide his dick in halfway, moving his waist in circular motions to open her up even more. Then he would thrust himself all the way inside of her, his balls slapping against her ass as he did so. She screamed in ecstasy. The feeling was too much. The pain was sweet, the joy sweeter, but this was more than she had ever handled before in her life. She tried to run away, but he leaned back, grabbing her thighs and throwing her legs over his shoulders, making her canal even more accessible. She knew she wasn't going anywhere now except for on a very wild ride.

He was so glad that she was flexible, because he had every intention of turning this cute little pretzel out. With her legs across his shoulders, he leaned forward, sucking her breasts, turning her on more and more with each lick. She grabbed his head: he knew her spot. She dug her nails into his scalp and back as he kissed, licked and sucked first one nipple, then the other, all the while increasing the tempo of his thrusts. His ass bounced in the air as he started to piston in and out of her pussy, the sounds of their sex and her increasingly wet love box filling the room. Her moans and his grunts joined the sound of their lovemaking as he continued to stretch her through multiple levels of pleasure.

Amidst the incredible orgasm that was building inside of her, she managed a smile: she had a sudden urge for Lucky Charms. His sex was so good that it had her seeing yellow stars, purple moons, green clovers and gold condom wrappers. She hugged him closer to her, working her vaginal muscles to try and pull and force his cum from his body. Alas, that was not what he had in mind. Instead he grabs her ass firmly and flips their sexual puzzle over, leaving her straddling his erection and his back lying on the bed. She didn't miss a beat, starting to ride his dick like a professional cowgirl. She could feel his rather large penis massaging all of her inner walls and it pleased her so. Her juices were running down the length of his shaft and down his thighs. Lovely.

The passion heating the room took a turn for the hotter as her grinding became more intense. She was so close to orgasm and she could tell that he was also by the stiffening of his dick, which she hadn't known was even possible. He pinched her nipples, so sensitive to his touch and that set off a series of fireworks within her loins. That, coupled with her clit rubbing against his firm lower abdomen, sent her over the precipice. She screamed for him to fuck her, hard. He moved his hands so that he could reach under her thighs and grab her soft ass, raising his hips as he did so, pounding her pussy from below. He couldn't even claim to be in Heaven right now. He was well beyond that. His balls were swelling against her ass, eager to release their load. She leaned forward, grabbing his pecs in her hands, needing something, anything, to hold on to as the first intense wave of her climax rocked her body.

She threw any and all inhibition to the wind, screaming his name as loud as she could, not caring about anyone or anything else in the world. He shared that sentiment as he erupted into her, nearly blacking out from the force of it all. He brought his hands around her back, needing her close to him as he involuntarily spasmed ounce after ounce of his seed into her, her body giving as much as she took in. Neither wanted to let the other go, which was fitting: neither could even if they did want to. They stayed frozen like this...one minute, two minutes, until their spasms eventually subsided and their bucking ceased. They looked into each other's eyes and knew they were thinking the same thing: that was the best that either had ever had, which was interesting, seeing as it was their first time.

First Date Sex, pt 1

Sarah was surprised. Chris did everything right on this date. She wasn't usually fond of blind dates but her friends really hooked her up on this one. Chris was attractive, masculine in all the right ways, a gentleman (opening doors for her and such...whew!) and had the greatest sense of humor. There was just one more test that he had to pass before she would give him her heart. She didn't normally do anything on the first date other than a brief hug and maybe allow a peck on the cheek if the guy played all his cards right. But, there was NEVER anything further than that...until now.

Chris handled himself in such a way that Sarah found herself wet before they finished their first few frames of bowling. He had a certain style about his person that she was finding irresistible. She could tell that he liked what he saw in her as well. She was attractive and she knew it. She just chose not to flaunt it. Usually those actions led to much unwanted attention.

They left the bowling alley, innocently grazing hands. They played the game: sort of holding hands, kind of not. It was cute. Sarah wanted much more than cute tonight. Before they even left the parking lot, she knew she had to have him and she had to have all of him. She remembered earlier in the evening that he had mentioned something about being sensitive around his neck and ears. So, she made it her business to touch him lightly around his neck, sliding her soft fingers down his hairline and along his right ear, feeling the hairs on his neck rise. Yes, she was getting a rise out of him.

Chris wasn't expecting much to happen tonight, at least not physically. But, he knew this game, and he knew where it would most likely lead. He didn't like to assume things when it came to women, especially not when it came to sex. However, Sarah had leaned over and was whispering interestingly naughty things in his ear. He had to remember to thank their mutual friends in the morning after they woke up because he knew he'd be sleeping in.

By the time Chris pulled up to her downtown apartment, Sarah was kissing and licking fervently on his ear, finding herself straining against the urge to tug on his pants zipper. Chris hurriedly put the car in park on the side of her street and turned to her, her tongue moving up to meet his as they met in a passionate kiss. She was beautiful, she was exotic and she was a hell of a kisser. Could he ask for more?

Apparently, he could because she began tugging on his zipper. Sarah didn't know what had come over her, but she knew she had to have as much of him as possible. The way he walked up to the lane in the bowling alley, it was as if his dick was too big for his body, which added sexiness to his walk. She was excited and couldn't wait to see it.

Chris couldn't believe what was happening. He could tell early on that Sarah was feeling him and he figured that eventually they would get to this point, but not on the first night. If he wasn't as interested in other aspects of her personality, this would have been a turn-off. However, that wasn't the case with her...at ALL.

She managed to finally get his erection out of his pants, struggling a bit because he was blessed down there. That was exactly what she wanted to see. So, he passed the first test in her mind, as she couldn't even fit her hand all the way around his staff. She began the second test and she leaned closer to his member.

"Oh...wow!" was all that he could exclaim. She got straight to business, deciding to use both of her hands to handle that snake. She pursed her lips as she brought him closer to her mouth to simulate her tight pussy. If Chris passed all three tests tonight, he'd be inside her pussy for real later on. He'd already passed two...

Chris placed his right hand on the back of her head without meaning to. It just felt so good, the way she worked her hands firmly up and down his dick felt like he was inside of a hot pussy. He couldn't believe this. Three minutes in and she was already the best he'd ever had. She was a pro and he loved it. One moment she was firm with her grasps, and then she was sliding her hands up and down his shaft, steadily trying to pump him. He loved her determination. He had never experienced an orgasm from oral sex before, but something told him this time would be different. And just a few moments later, he was right.

Sarah had no previous knowledge of Chris' inexperience with cumming from getting head, but she could tell that he was about to have one now. His shaft, already rock hard, got even harder still as she took one hand off his dick and began to massage his balls. She could taste the pre-cum beginning to leak from the tip of his dick and she was ready for the load. She went back to her two-handed technique and sucked Chris' dick for all she was worth.

Chris put both of his hands on the steering wheel, holding on for dear life, it seemed. He'd busted plenty of nuts before, but never had he felt a rush like this! Sarah reached across him and hit the seat lever, pushing him back until his seat reclined all the way back. She didn't want any obstructions as she conducted this final test.

Chris was forced to let go of the steering wheel when Sarah reclined his seat and had nothing to hold on to as his impending orgasm rushed up from his loins. So he just folded his hands over his face and braced for it. He was about to blow!

Sarah knew it was just a matter of seconds, so she continued her suck fest, stroking him up and down, wet kisses to the tip, flicking her tongue around the head of his dick and around the base of his shaft. When she felt the cum flowing up his shaft, she placed his penis all the way in her mouth, deep throating him so that he could cum in her mouth and have it flow straight down her throat.

Chris couldn't control himself! This is what he had been missing?! He moaned loudly, his hands unknowingly gripping the back of her head as he jerked and spasmed each drop of semen into her mouth. Once the initial bursts slowed down, she began stroking him again, squeezing each ounce of his love juice to the tip of his dick and licking it off. It was so sweet! Yes! Sarah was amazed. He had passed all of her tests. He had a great personality, he was a gentleman, and he had an amazing cock. Well, there was just ONE more test...the biggie. How could she forget?

She finished him off, making sure there was no more sweet juice to be had. Once he was flaccid again, she helped him back into his boxers and jeans and zipped them for him. Chris raised his seat back up and sighed...wow.

"So," Sarah asked, "I think we need to continue this upstairs. What do you think?" She began laughing as she finished her statement, because Chris was already unlocking his door and exiting the vehicle. Oh, and how sweet: he opened her door for her.

First Date Sex, pt 2

Chris was beyond excited. He let Sarah drag him to her apartment. She'd have had an easier time if he knew where she lived, but he didn't, not yet. He was only seconds away, though. He still couldn't believe what had just happened. His dick was still slightly erect from just the thought of Sarah's lips wrapped around him in the front seat of his car. He just HAD to return the favor and he couldn't wait.

They finally made it upstairs to Sarah's apartment and she quickly excused herself to the restroom to freshen up. She wanted to go all out and see exactly what Chris would go for. While she was washing and rinsing her girl parts, Chris strolled around the apartment. The couch was nice and plush. Good, that would be comfortable to dig her out on. The floor was carpeted. He leaned down, rubbing it: soft. Good, that'll decrease the chance of severe rug burns on their knees. He took a quick peek in her bedroom: tidy. Good, he didn't want to be tripping over furniture as he carried her in there to finish their wild romp.

Sarah exited the bathroom, wearing nothing but her bra. She figured he was going to see it all sooner rather than later, so what was the point of hiding it now? Besides, she was entirely too horny to be playing "Hide and Go Get It." She skipped over to a wide eyed Chris, kissing his lips hard before breaking away and breathlessly asking if he was ready for round two.

Chris' response was to pick Sarah up right there in the middle of the living room and continue lifting her until she was sitting on his face with her hands wrapped around his back! This was impressive due to the fact that Chris was still standing and didn't appear to be unbalanced in any way. Due to his height and her stance atop his face and shoulders, Sarah was able to steady herself by pushing her hands against the living room ceiling. This was a first!

They'd gone out earlier to grab something to eat before bowling but it seemed as if Chris hadn't eaten for weeks by the way his tongue was digging inside of her increasingly wet pussy. Sarah was in heaven, and her proximity to the ceiling helped increase the effect. She was caught between digging her fingernails in his scalp as a result of his mouth ravaging her sweetness and continuing her press against the ceiling. Sarah didn't want to fall but she was forgetting more about the ceiling with each thrust of his tongue and loving his oral skills.

Chris felt like he was eating the sweetest peach cobbler. Sarah's pussy was so sweet and juicy. He had a strong stance going and wasn't worried about dropping her. In addition to a wide base, he had both hands firmly planted on her ass, each cheek being grabbed by one of his strong hands.

Sarah reached down, confident in Chris' abilities to hold her up with little to no effort, and began rubbing her hands and nails in his hair and scalp. This turned him on so much; he loved getting his head rubbed! He turned his body and effortlessly tossed Sarah onto her plush couch. Sarah sat up as Chris got down on bended knee and pulled her legs over his shoulders, giving his tongue and lips greater access to her juice box.

Sarah moaned aloud in pleasure as Chris continued dining on her sweet feast. She loved the way he lightly kissed her clit and swirled his tongue around it, increasing her pleasure a thousand fold as she pushed herself against his face, wanting him to swallow every ounce of juice she gave him. She especially loved the way he trailed his tongue from her pussy to her ass and back, kissing along the way. Ooh, a freak!

Sarah couldn't hold back anymore. She was on the verge of exploding and her stomach was tightening, that tell-tell sign that she was about to cum. Maybe now would be a good time to warn Chris that she was a...

It was too late! Chris couldn't believe it! Sarah was a squirter! He tried as hard as he could to catch and swallow every drop of love juice that her pussy threw at him. He knew right then and then that the two of them were a perfect match. He laughed to himself as her body quivered and jumped each time he sucked on her clit and kissed her lips as she rode her orgasm.

Finally Sarah was able to calm down and relax as Chris continued to kiss up and down her thighs, allowing her a chance to regain her composure. She opened her eyes and fell heavily in lust with the sight in front of her. Somewhere during that episode, Chris had taken his shirt off and what a sight he was! She leaned forward, kissing his chest and rubbing his arms before she stood up, grabbing his hands. She led him into her bedroom; it was time to do the ultimate...

First Date Sex, pt 3

Sarah was excited. This night had gone nowhere near as planned and she couldn't be happier. Chris had a fun personality, a great sense of humor and a big dick. On top of all that, he ate pussy like a champ!

Chris was stoked. He couldn't believe that tonight was going the way that it was but he couldn't have been any happier if he tried. Actually, as he watched Sarah get on her bed in the doggystyle position, he realized that he could get much happier and he was well on his way to making sure she felt the same.

Chris stepped behind her, admiring the spectacular view in front of him. Her ass was full and supple, and her pussy was winking at him. He placed his hands on her hips and aimed the head of his dick for her wet slit, the blood racing through his body. Sarah looked back at him as she pushed her ass against him, her pussy opening up as he pushed his way into her.

Sarah let out a moan as euphoria overtook her, Chris' dick filling her up completely. She was amazed at how full her pussy felt and Chris was amazed at how wet she remained. She was so tight and warm. He had to ease in slowly; he didn't want to blow his load before he had a chance to get as deep as possible. He squeezed her ample ass and pushed himself into her, deeper and deeper until his dick couldn't go any further.

Sarah's moans became louder and louder as Chris slid his thickness into her and out of her, picking up the speed and strength of his thrusts. She loved the way his balls slapped against her clit and the sound his thighs made as he slid into her with each powerful, orgasmic thrust. She couldn't contain her excitement and the pleasure that was racing through her body.

This was heaven. The way their bodies moved with each other and the intensity they felt as they fucked was amazing. Sarah looked back at Chris with insane desire in her eyes and licked her lips, which was enough to push Chris into another realm. He drew back, taking his penis all the way out of her dripping wet pussy and drove himself into her, mad with intense lust.

The force with which he began fucking her sent Sarah over the precipice. She began to cum, over and over, her body starting to shake heavily. She couldn't believe dick this good existed. Chris was easily placed atop her list of all time favorites. If they were in Vegas, she would marry this man right now and then fuck him on the altar! His sex game was vicious.

Sarah lay flat on her stomach, her legs still spread as Chris continued to punish her pussy in the best way possible. She reached behind her with both of her hands and spread her ass cheeks so that Chris could see himself sliding in and out of her wetness.

It was too much! Chris couldn't contain himself when he saw Sarah's juices glistening on his erection. Watching her pussy lips suck on his dick put him over. He could feel his semen beginning to rush forth from his balls and race up his shaft.

"Cum on my ass, baby!" was all she could manage to scream as another orgasm rocked her body. She knew from experience that he was about to cum as his already incredibly rock hard dick got even harder and thicker. Feeling that stiffness inside her walls made her cum again, her pussy squirting all over her sheets.

At that exclamation from Sarah and the squirting he felt against his nuts, Chris pulled out just as he busted a huge load all over her ass and back. Sarah pushed her ass higher in the air, catching all of him. Chris had to use a hand to steady himself as the intensity of his orgasm rocked his body.

Sarah loved the warmth of his seed all over her back. That shit was sexy. She looked back behind her to see Chris, eyes closed, dick in hand. She got up and turned around racing to take his dick into her mouth. She caught him off guard as she sucked him greedily; making sure all of his seed went down her throat. Succulent!

She finished polishing him off as he massaged her breasts, turning her on again. She swallowed the last little drop of him and got up to clean up. She returned with a hot rag and wiped him down as well. She looked into his glazed over eyes and she could tell that this was the start of a very hot relationship. He kissed her in agreement.

Car Sexin'

Diana couldn't believe it; she had never done something like this before. She was actually sitting in the front seat of this man's car and she'd only just laid eyes on him a few minutes ago. She was feeling such a rush right now. She'd never gotten in a car with a stranger before, never with the explicit intent of having sex with them.

Well, maybe she shouldn't consider him a stranger, right? After all, they'd been talking, chit-chatting, communicating on various social networking sites for almost a year now. They'd exchanged pics, talked on the phone and gotten to know each other quite well. However, in this day and age you never could tell with some people. That's why Diana made sure to pack her box cutter and mace in her purse.

However, as soon as she stepped in the car and saw Mike's smile, she knew she was in good hands. And she hoped that in a few minutes, a good dick would be inside her. Yes, this was their first actual encounter with each other, but they knew exactly was this was supposed to be. Neither one was looking for a relationship. Mike wanted some wet pussy before he hit the road and Diana wanted a hard, long dick inside of her. She needed this nut. It had been almost a year since she had last had sex and she was a fiend right now.

She got in, buckled up and they were off. They continued various strains of conversations past as she directed Mike to a secluded spot near her apartment. She lived with her sister until she got her own place and there was NO way she was having sex there. Her sister was insanely old fashioned and paid the rent, so she had to abide by the rules. But it was ok; having sex in a public would be such a turn-on, even if it was almost midnight.

They finally arrived at a quiet spot near an empty house up the street. Mike pulled into the driveway and cut the lights. He'd had sex in a car before but it was a long time ago and he was paranoid of the cops showing up. That paranoia was soon displaced by euphoria as Diana took his dick out of his shorts and placed it in her mouth, the warmth causing his erection to fill her mouth and cover her tongue.

Mike let out a moan and started to recline his seat, but Diana stopped him. Sliding his dick out of her mouth with enough friction to cause it to exit with a pop, she started to get out of the car. Mike was confused until he saw her pulling down her shorts as she walked to the hood of his car and lifting her blouse and taking off her bra, releasing her ample breasts. Ah, he got it!

He quickly jumped out of the car and joined her in front of his car. They kissed passionately as she stroked his shaft, his erection heating up her hand. She broke the kiss and turned around, bending over the hood of his Altima, her ass pushed out and her pussy waiting for him to enter. Mike quickly lowered his pants, threw on the Magnum Ecstasy condom and entered Diana, but not with ease. Her pussy was so wet but so tight. Diana moaned aloud, surprising herself with the noise. She had momentarily forgotten that there were people around in the surrounding houses. She knew her pussy was going to be tight and she knew Mike was rather "blessed" off of the pictures that he had sent her, but she wasn't expecting it to this tight of a fit. But it felt oh so good. Mike slid his way into her, working his dick back and forth, her sex juices coating him as he slid in and out of her.

Diana put all of her weight on the hood of the car and reached both of her hands around to spread the cheeks of her ass so that her pussy would open up just a little bit more for Mike and his engorged member. It felt so good to be filled up by a hard, thick dick after such a long time.

Finally Mike was completely in her, his balls against her clit. She pushed her ass back against him, encouraging him to fuck her. He got the hint and started to stroke her pussy, picking up the tempo as her pussy sucked on his dick. This was even better than he could have imagined! He ducked down at one point when a neighbor from down the street drove by but that only increased his desire. Diana was trying to hold in her moans but that was only making him hotter. He wanted her to moan and scream. He wanted the world to know that he was fucking her outside, right next to their houses.

Diana couldn't hold back and didn't want to. She pushed her ass against him, giving as good as she was getting, her juices splashing against his thighs. She couldn't remember ever being this wet! Mike went into overdrive, fucking her with every ounce of his being and a few moments later he could feel his balls starting to swell, that tell-tell sign that he was about to cum.

Diana could feel his dick surging in girth and although it had been a while, she knew what that meant. She pushed back against him harder, forcing him out of her. She turned around quickly and jumped on the hood, spreading her legs. She wanted to look in his eyes as he came and wrap her legs around him. This was intense!

Mike moved back as she repositioned herself on the hood and laid back, her legs spread and her pussy wide for him. He entered her again, this time palming her breasts as well. Her titties were so thick and juicy that he couldn't help but to explode. He could feel her pussy sucking on him, as if she was trying to get every ounce of strength out of him.

His orgasm was hard and intense, as was hers. She'd already cum twice by now but the addition of his ejaculation heightened her third one and they both exploded. He leaned down, unable to stand fully and lightly bit her shoulder. Her pussy was exquisite. He continued to cum and she continued to flex her pussy muscles on his staff, squeezing everything out of him.

Finally, he was spent, but he wanted more. He stood up and slid out of her, taking the condom off as he did so. Wiping his brow, he looked at her and thought: maybe this shouldn't just be a sex thing? She winked at him, agreeing.

Mile High

I was nervous at first. I'd never been on a plane before. I had to fly out to Denver from Norfolk for a work conference and the only way out there was to fly. Dammit. I wasn't scared of flying, but since I hadn't done it before, I was nervous. Nervous until I met Tony.

It was a red-eye leaving at midnight and the plane was nearly empty. I don't know how I felt about that. Part of me wanted to feel safe knowing there were others sharing my plight and part of me didn't want others around to crowd me. Tony was in the seat directly across the aisle from me and smiled as soon as he sat down, and a beautiful smile it was. His teeth were perfect, a radiant white and even. Beautiful.

We exchanged pleasantries and locked in, waiting for the plane to take off. I listened intently to the flight attendant give the pre flight safety instructions, as I had never heard them before and was going to be prepared should anything happen. Safest way to travel, my ass.

Tony seemed much more at ease on the flight than I did. He glanced over at me a few times and smiled, surprisingly calming me down each time. Hmm...maybe I should keep that smile focused on me the whole flight; that way I won't have to think about anything else. He was wearing a nice casual outfit, light sweater, softly pressed jeans, loafers. He looked relaxed and comfortable, like he flies all the time.

I hadn't known it, but I found out that I was staring. I found out because he looked over at me for the thousandth time and I was right in his face...from across the aisle! I was so embarrassed! Not only was I staring, but my panties had seemingly found a leak somewhere in my pants. Where in the world did THAT come from?

"Are you feeling alright," he asked me. I was feeling fine, just fine, with the exception that I wanted to jump on him and ride him harder than any turbulence that could possibly be felt by the pilots up front.

"Y-yes, I'm fine, thank you," I stumbled. I couldn't believe the effect this man was having on me. I didn't even know him or anything about him but I was so tempted to do all manner of lascivious things to him. That would really take my mind off of the building pressure in my ears.

He smiled again. Damn, this man could get a contract with Crest, his teeth were so white! I think I started staring again, because my panties were about to burst open with the impending juices and he started laughing.

"I'm sorry. I am being rude. I don't mean to stare, it's just that..." I stopped myself. There was NO way that I was going to tell this strange man that I wanted to see what was in his jeans.

"Do you mind if I sit next to you," he asked, ignoring the awkward pause in my statement, "so that we're not speaking across the aisle like this for the entire flight?" I nodded my approval. I moved into the window seat, letting him sit in the one I had just previously occupied.

We talked more as the plane ascended into the night air, unknowingly getting closer and closer as our voices turned down so as to not be heard, even though there were only like four other people on the plane and maybe two attendants.

Somewhere in the middle of the flight, after discussing life goals and silly childhood moments, the topic turned to sex. I was fairly naive when it came to sex; the most open place being the living room couch in my parent's house when they went on an anniversary vacation when I was in college. I had never done anything bold or daring. That wasn't my style, but that's because I had never really messed with any guys that were adventurous. I didn't feel like I was missing anything, though.

He asked me, "Have you ever heard of the Mile High Club?"

"Sure!" I may have been inexperienced in the matters wild, but I had some basic knowledge.

"You ever considered joining?" That took me by surprise. Was this man serious? I couldn't believe my ears. Was he propositioning me right here, 30,000 feet in the air, for sex?! I was shocked at that, taken aback, even.

"I am now." I was even more surprised at my answer.

Without another word, he took my hand and quickly led me back to the lavatory, opening the door and ushering me inside. I felt like such a kink! I couldn't believe I was about to do this! I felt lightheaded at the sudden rush of adrenaline that was racing through my body. I was doing this. I was really doing this.

Tony closed the door behind him and smiled that gorgeous smile. I didn't know if he had done this before and I didn't care. I wanted to get started before I lost my nerve. I pulled him across the very small space we had toward me and kissed him, harder than I meant to. I eased up a little just so I could say that I actually enjoyed the kiss. I did enjoy it, too. His breath was amazingly fresh and his tongue slid into my mouth effortlessly and with no more force than necessary. Ooh, a gentle lover, hmm?

I was so thankful that I had decided on a skirt, because that was going to make this a lot easier. "Tear my panties off, now," I panted, his kisses enflaming my desire. They were already useless to me, as I had soaked them with pussy juice.

"I want to taste you, baby." He looked into my eyes and licked his lips. Since most guys didn't seem like they wanted to lick the box, I was tempted to let him, but I was starting to lose my nerve with each moment that he wasn't inside me.

"We don't really have the time or space for that, you think?"

He nodded quickly, agreeing as he wrestled with my Vickie's and turning me on as he did so, his fingers rubbing against my clitoris and pussy lips. I know he could feel just how juicy I was. I wanted this so badly. The sensation of being in a public place, with others right outside the door and his fingers now massaging my clit had me on tilt! I needed is hardness inside of me!

I fumbled with his zipper, no easy task, and finally was able to release the beast from within his boxer briefs. He was already semi erect and it was gorgeous. I shared his sentiment because I wanted that dick in my mouth just as much as he wanted my pussy in his. I held strong, though, just as he lifted me a few inches in the air and slid me onto his shaft, my legs wrapping around his waist.

I tried to help the situation by bracing my hands against the wall as he slid in and out of my juiciness. I wanted to keep my moans to a minimum, but I just couldn't help it. He filled me up and I could feel my pussy stretching around him. Oh, this pleasure was so divine! His dick was perfect and felt as if it were molded to fit my box and mine alone. His hands gripped on my ass, spreading my cheeks with each thrust.

"Oh, god...Tony!" I knew I was getting loud, but at this point, I refused to care. It was heaven, which was fitting, given our position in the skies.

I placed one shoe on the edge of the toilet and leaned back against the wall, allowing him deeper access. I wanted it all, and the sex in my eyes demanded. He leaned back against the door and pushed against my pussy. Good, he could read sex.

His hands on my hips, he began pushing harder and further into me, his balls slapping against my ass, more and more or my wetness coating his dick. I loved it! I grabbed the back of his head and scratched his neck, oblivious to everything beside the pressure building up within me. I was close to orgasm, tearfully close.

I began to fuck him back, bucking my hips against him, causing his erection to go deeper and deeper into me. I wanted to explode all over his dick and then lick it off.

Before long, I couldn't hold it in any longer. I arched my back as he continued to drill me, my cream squirting all over his cock and pants. I felt no shame, only sweet blessed relief as I continued to cum all over him and myself. I had never squirted before. He looked down, beaming. I'm glad he didn't mind the impending stain.

The look in his eyes quickly turned to one of supposed pain, and I knew he was holding back. I pushed him out of me and sat down on the commode, his dick directly in front of me. Wasting no time, I took him into my mouth, stroking his thickness with both hands and swirling my tongue around the tip of his penis, where I knew most of the nerve endings were. Thank goodness for Sexual Health class.

I was determined to make this man feel an orgasm as strong as the one I had just experienced and I didn't fail myself. He grabbed the back of my head, shoving himself almost the hilt. I gagged slightly but held on as he started to erupt, his hot seed flying to the back of my throat. I was getting turned on again by that alone. He held my head still as he continued to release himself inside of me, his dick slowly becoming flaccid. I began sucking him off again, making sure that I took in every last drop. He was delicious. I had never given a blowjob like that before.

"Wow," he said, finally, after catching his breath, "I've never gotten a blowjob like that before." I giggled. This was the most daring thing that I had ever done. I couldn't believe myself, but I wasn't ashamed. But then, there was a knock on the door...

Do It Like It's The First Time, pt 1

Her eyes are spellbinding, like you'd see on an exotic Persian woman. I couldn't turn away except to gaze at the ink on her shoulders: mesmerizing and punk at the same time. I knew this would make for an excellent experience. I managed to break away from her eyes long enough to linger on her lips, envisioning them wrapped around my shaft, long and hard, going in and out, in and out of her warm and welcoming mouth. Coincidentally, that is exactly what she was doing, and I couldn't take my eyes off of hers. The way she looked up at me while she serviced me with her mouth, her lips pouty and full, turned me on. I was caught up.

You have to understand how much I loved the way she looked at me when we did our thing. When I was between her thighs, her eyes looked down on me with the sexiest and fiercest gaze, as if she wanted me to swallow her whole. When we were fucking, her hazel and brown eyes glowed with raw emotion. I knew what that look meant, "Fuck me, take me, consume me." She never had to say it. I just knew. And when she performed fellatio on me, her look was all love. She wanted me to be pleased, and pleased I was during every moment.

I had to contain myself just a bit so as to not go overboard but I couldn't help but to guide myself in and out of her mouth by grabbing her by the back of her head and neck. I managed to break eye contact long enough for them to roll to the back of my skull. My goodness, this was amazing head! She knew exactly how to suck me off, licking my shaft from the very tip all the way to the base, never neglecting my balls. She rubbed my chest with whatever free hand she had while she kissed and sucked on me just like I liked it.

I was so close to orgasm, but I didn't want to end in this way, not yet. I slid out of her mouth, somewhat reluctantly, and stood her up, placing kisses along her mouth and neck as I guided her back toward her bed. I always enjoyed the way she pleasured me with her mouth and now it was my turn to please her.

She looked at me with those piercing eyes, knowing what was to come. She kissed me, hard, before lying back on the bed and slowly spreading herself open to me. My dick jumped in anticipation, but it wasn't time for that yet. My mouth watered. It was definitely time for that.

She inched back further and further until her back was against the headboard while I crawled to her, licking my lips with desire. I reached her and immediately began my feast, spreading her lips with my tongue as I first ignored her clit and dove into her pussy, probing as far as that muscle could go. She responded with an excited gasp and grabbed my head, pulling my face deeper into her essence. I could feel my dick throbbing against the mattress, that's how much the taste of her turned me on.

She was breathtaking. If you could just imagine the purest honey mixed with the sweetest milk, that's what she was to me. I lapped hungrily, like a lion cub with his first meal. She always tells me that for her, the best part of me performing cunnilingus on her wasn't as much the act (although she loved that); it was that I got so into it. I couldn't help it; she tasted like what I expected Heaven to be like: divine. I kissed her from the opening of her juice box to the hood of her clit, licking and sucking along the way, garnering gasps and moans from the head of the bed. Her moans turned me on, but I wanted to hear her scream.

She liked it when I was gentle, but she loved it when I got a little rough. She liked the intensity and I loved the fire that she emitted. I nibbled ever so lightly on her inner labia, and she squeezed her thighs against my head in response. I placed a finger across the top of her clitoral hood and began rubbing and pushing against it while I sucked on her pussy hole. Just as I intended, she went insane. She wrapped her legs around my neck and back and we both knew that there was no returning.

She began grinding her hips against me, silently begging me to go harder. She was a freak after my own heart and I wanted to push the boundaries further. I could feel her ankles locked together on my back, pressing down into me as I sucked on her clit, pulling it from under its hood with my tongue. I held her right thigh with my left arm as I began to finger her pussy with the already slick fingers of my right hand, sliding first one and then two and three fingers inside her. She ground her pussy against me harder, moaning my name as I worked her feverishly toward an orgasm. I sucked and licked harder, stopping occasionally to bite her inner thigh. I wanted to leave my mark.

I also wanted her to bless me with the waters of her loins. I pressed two fingers deep inside her and managed to turn her over onto her stomach with my fingers still inside. This sensation caused her to cum for the first time, the first of many. With her ass in the air and my fingers inside her, I gave in to the urge to slap her ass with my now free left hand. She had fair and light skin and bruised easily, but she enjoyed the pain. I slapped her ass repeatedly while I licked all over her nether regions, enjoying the way she shook while under my control. She pushed her ass against my face, groaning and writhing in ecstasy. I was so turned on and it showed in the way that I finger fucked her while eating her ass and pussy out.

The point came where we couldn't take anymore of this teasing. She needed to be filled completely and I needed to fill her. I pushed her against the headboard as I kneeled behind her, reaching around to pinch her nipples as I entered her tightness. It amazed me how she managed to stay so tight and strong on me.

Do It Like It's The First Time, pt 2

My hips thrust forward as my head rocked back. My god, her vagina was heaven-sent! I knew those blasphemies would land me a first class ticket to hell but she made it feel like it was worth it! I grabbed her hips for leverage as she started throwing herself back onto me. It became a competition to see who could thrust harder. I knew that I was going to lose because I could already feel cum surging up the length of my dick.

She felt it too, and I knew she was close by the way her pussy started tightening around me and spasming uncontrollably.

We both let loose into and onto each other, our lascivious passion mixing and dripping onto the sheets beneath us. I was so weak and collapsed on top of her back, but my erection was still standing strong. She bucked her ass back forcefully, pushing me out of her before turning around pushing me onto my back. Yes! She was about to take control. She licked my dick again, sucking the creamy mixture that was our cum off of me. I found myself getting even more turned on at the sight of her licking and sucking on something that was coated in her juices. I loved a woman that loved the way she tasted.

After nearly bringing me to another orgasm simply by sucking on me, she straddled me, fire in her eyes. This was going to get rough, just how we liked it. She commenced to bouncing on my dick, proclaiming how much she loved the feel and taste of my cock and how it was going to belong to her forever. I took my eyes off of her bouncing tits long enough to agree, knowing that she got off on her power over me.

Eventually she found herself weak from the action and came all over my dick again, leaning forward to kiss me and suck on my tongue. I wrapped my hands around her and rubbed her neck before sliding my nails down her back. Her nipples were pressed against mine as she shivered, enjoying the mix of pleasure and pain that coursed through her body.

While still rock hard inside her, I switched our positions, placing me in a standard of power. It was my turn to be the master. At this point during our sessions, nothing was off limits. Nothing was taboo. Nothing was forsaken.

"Whose pussy is this?" I teased her by pulling out of her almost all of the way, only the head of my penis still inside. She whimpered in response. I slammed my dick back inside of her dripping wetness and asked again, with more force and authority. "Whose pussy is this?!"

"Yours, papi," was her meek response. Good girl. I rewarded her with three painstakingly slow strokes. She moaned again. "Please fuck me...please," she whined into the air. She had a love/hate relationship with this torture. She wanted the dick, and she wanted all of it now. But she also wanted to be teased. I could give her both. That's what made up part of our dynamic.

"You'll get fucked when I'm ready to fuck you," was my response, coupled with me leaning down and biting on her nipples. I started with the left one and then the right, but not too hard. First I kissed them with my lips before grazing her nipples with my teeth as I licked around her areola. I steadily and slowly applied pressure until I heard her moan and felt her jump. I could feel her pussy getting wetter as well. She came again.

At this point, she was rubbing and scratching my back, leaving trails of broken skin. It hurt like fire but it made me hot. I wanted her to continue but I wanted her to have as little mobility as possible. I walked my hands up her arms, forcing them above her head and then holding both of them in my large grasp with one hand. With the other hand, I walked back down her right arm and landed on her neck.

Her breathing became shallow as she became even more excited. She loved this part and made sure to tell me every time. I placed my left hand around the front of her neck and squeezed ever so slightly, smiling inside at the sudden gasp that she emitted. She wound her legs around mine and closed her eyes and I slowly increased the pressure of both my hold on her neck and the depth in which I was entering her canal below.

I increased my pace and fervor as I held onto her neck, squeezing harder and harder. She responded by bucking her hips into me. I released my grip just as the faintest hint of a tear smiled at the corner of her eyes, and as soon as she took a much needed, albeit stubborn, gasp of air, the pressure was back on.

I could barely understand the words coming out of her mouth what with me choking on her, my grunts in the air and her moans filling the room, but I knew she was trying to tell me to fuck her harder. And fuck her I did.

To get leverage for the final push I released the hold on her neck and sat back, lifting both of her legs in the air and placing them over my shoulders. I leaned forward until her knees were almost beside her head and commenced to stroking away, harder and harder. I leaned forward just a little bit more to lick her lips and suck on her tongue as we raced to the finish line, aching to see who would cum the hardest.

She grabbed the back of my head, pulling me closer to her as she forced her tongue in my mouth. She was helpless to move her waist or hips but I could feel her trying to fuck me just like I was fucking her: hard and fast.

I leaned back as I felt her pussy tightening on me because I wanted to look in her eyes as she came on me. She lifted her ass off of the bed as she crossed her threshold, her hands caught up in the sheets and blankets that she was grabbing. I loved it when she had one of those "earth shattering" orgasms because it meant I did my job.

Watching her cum all over my dick and the subsequent juices spill onto the sheets gave me a rush and I sped toward my second finish. Right as her spasms began to subside, I grabbed her hips, still lifted off of the mattress and began to fuck her almost violently, wanting to spill my seed all over her.

As I reached my sexual zenith and pulled out of her, she reached up quickly and took me into her mouth, causing my already sensitive organ to explode. Without a care as to who could possibly hear me, I moaned aloud as stream after stream of my semen flew into her mouth. She swallowed as much as she could, the rest filling her mouth and spilling out of the corners of her lips. I grabbed the back of her head without knowing it and essentially began fucking her face until I was well spent.

After I crested my last wave, I leaned back, breathless. She left me and came from the bathroom with a hot cloth. The heat from the water and the touch of the material felt so exquisite. I could feel myself getting aroused again...

The Head Nurse

Her face, perfectly made up (though a touch heavy on the eyeliner), was home to a very full and very sexy set of lips. With my imagination in overdrive as I sat in the hospital waiting room for two hours, I imagined her walking over to me and kneeling. I could see her perfectly manicured nails walking a trail of lust up my thighs and releasing my belt buckle. She looks at me, smiles. Her teeth are even, white, magnificent. She finds my cock with ease but has the slightest bit of difficulty in freeing it from its denim prison, as my erection is growing rapidly by the second. She kisses the tip of the head before blessing me by wrapping her tongue around me and sliding along the length of my shaft. I moan aloud, oblivious to the persons around me. They take no notice of us either: her with one hand wrapped around the base of my dick and the other massaging my balls; me with eyes closed and both hands cupping the base of her head, pulling her deeper onto me. Soon she is in full mode and her actions become faster and more intense. She takes in all of me, down to the hilt and then slides all the way up, teasing my dick but for a moment before deep throating me again. Her skill is undeniable as she pushes me...no, forces me to climax. I nearly cry with pleasure as she swallows my seed, never stopping or even slowing her care giving. She drains the last of my life creating essence and I am spent. I open my eyes only to see her walk away with another patient. I open the newspaper that is in my lap and sigh. Damn this imagination of mine.

Lunchtime Special

Time couldn't go on fast enough. Alisha looked at the seconds tick by on the clock behind her, wondering if two o'clock would ever show up. She had a lunch date and she didn't want to be late. She had twenty minutes after class to run to her apartment, exchange her books for the next class and wash up before heading to her rendezvous point. And by then, they only had about an hour to chill.

He wasn't her boyfriend, and she was cool with that. What with college, maintaining friendships, keeping her grades and social networking up and working, Alisha didn't have time for relationships. She had barely enough time to hold onto her sanity and friendships while juggling everything else. Shit, she barely had enough time to meet up with this guy that she met in a club two months ago.

He provided a welcome release for her, though. He wasn't your typical male in the way that he approached her. Instead he was reserved, had manners, and was polite. By the end of that first night, she was willing to give him the cell number, silently praying that he didn't turn out to be some weird stalker. Heaven knows she needed NO drama.

Thankfully, he was drama free. He was easy to talk to, respectful, creative, open minded and a freak after her own heart. She made him wait a while before she let him sample the goods simply because she did have standards and wasn't giving a taste of that luscious ass up to just anybody. He seemed like he would make great boyfriend material given the amazing characteristics, but she was adamant with her heart on that one: love would have to wait.

Lust, however, did not. After a few weeks of feeling him and making sure he passed the Crazy Test, she was ready to feel him out in another fashion. She had seen the slight bulge in his pants on many occasions and had even felt it jump against her whenever they danced. She was more than curious to try it out.

She recalled their first encounter as a heated blush ran across her cheeks while she packed her book bag, the professor having had just released the class for the day after assigning more homework. Great.

Her mind was quickly taken off the nights impending work as she remembered going to his house about a month ago. The first couple times she had been there they just chilled but this one time was different. She went there knowing she was going to give it up. She had her next class at four o'clock and like today, didn't have as much time to devote to sex as she would have liked.

She remembered walking inside his apartment as she had done a few times before and walking directly to his bedroom. The confused look on his face was cute: they normally hung out in the living room.

"I have class in a little over an hour, so get to it." She didn't mean to come off as being so demanding, but before Alisha could apologize, he pushed her onto the bed.

"Don't rush me," he growled, "take your clothes off." Wow. This was a change in character but she found herself immediately turned on and wet. She scrambled to slide her pants down over her ample behind but she barely had the zipper down before he almost literally ripped her pants and panties down and off, slinging them across the room. Oh, their first time was going to be like this? Alisha's pussy: even wetter.

What happened next was even more surprising. She started to crab walk backwards on the bed toward the headboard, thinking they were about to get their sex on when he reached under her, grabbing her thighs and pulling her back toward him. He immediately buried his face in her love box, throwing every ounce of her all of the way off!

She couldn't focus her sight for the stars, stripes, flags, doves, flowers and balloons she saw before her. This man could eat some pussy! She felt like she was everywhere at once and couldn't control herself. She fell backwards, her hands alternating between grabbing the sheets and pulling on his hair. She found that she had no control over her thighs anymore, her hips quivering and pulsating as he licked, sucked and nibbled at her sweet pearl. One orgasm, two orgasms, three...

His tongue was a magnificent snake, sliding in and out of the pussy, slurping all of her juices and swallowing her fire. She grabbed the back of his head, pulling his tongue in deeper and deeper still. She hadn't had her sex muscles devoured like this in ages and it felt so exquisite. As she recalled this encounter she giggled to herself; she wondered if she started speaking in tongues?

She couldn't take it anymore and she was still mindful of the time, so she pushed his head in deeper, getting her juices all over his face and mouth before she pulled him back and off of her so he could get on the bed with her.

She didn't know if he expected to have the favor reciprocated, but she was far too horny to care about that. She wanted him in every way possible. She wanted to see and taste that delicious shaft that she had been imagining for so many days.

She lay him back while she began stroking on his already rock hard erection. His size and girth was impressive, very impressive. She remembered hoping for a split second that he knew what to do with all of that meat, but she knew now that he definitely knew how to work it.

She got her mouth ready for him and took him in, albeit with some effort. The man was blessed, she had to admit. She hadn't sucked on a dick or had sex in quite a while and she wanted to take her time but her lust pushed her forward. She continued to stroke him as she slobbed his dick, greasing him up for her pussy, which was already soaking wet.

She looked up at him to see his head tilted back, eyelids closed. He let out a long drawn out moan and his dick jumped so she knew she was doing something right. She sucked up his shaft while massaging his balls until he exited her mouth with a slight pop. His dick glistened in the afternoon sun. It was so beautiful. She wanted nothing more than to jump on it and after pulling out a condom she brought along for the occasion, she did.

He slid inside her with relative ease. She had the slightest bit of apprehension about her, it being her very first time on top during sex. Plus, it had been a while since she had gotten any. He opened his eyes and, looking into hers, grabbed her about her waist, slowly guiding her up and then down on his hardness. She leaned forward, her hands on his chest as she raised her ass up. She took in every aspect of this experience as her pussy slid back down on him, swallowing it, inch by inch. She leaned her head back, enjoying the way he filled her canal until it felt like the head of his dick was poking her cervix. God, so big and full!

She began to gain more and more confidence as she picked up her pace, her ass beginning to fly in the air. Up and down she thrust herself onto him, impaling herself on his cock, coming closer and closer to yet another orgasm.

She found herself disappointed when he pulled her off of him. He sated her desire when he put her in the doggystyle position and entered her from behind. She came instantly when he thrust the full power of his dick inside her, sending her juices all over his thighs. She recalls screaming his name, oblivious to the possibility of anyone else being in the house.

The pleasure coursing through her body was almost too much for her to handle but she hung on like a soldier, throwing her ass back onto him and giving as good as she got. The sounds of her ass slapping against him turned her on even more. That, coupled with his moans and grunts and the sweet smell of their sex in the air, launched her over the edge again.

She felt his dick getting harder still and she knew that he was close. His thrusts became stronger and harder as he grabbed her hips and ass tightly. She smirked to herself as she thought, there was a lot to grab back there. She was short but very proportionate. She looked back at him, making eye contact right before he let out a guttural roar. His body locked up as Alisha squeezed her pussy muscles tight, her moment of ecstasy colliding with his as they both spent themselves on and in each other.

He seemed to space out for the greater part of a minute. Damn, how long had it been since he had any? She carefully pulled off of him and turned around, sliding the condom off of his dick before kissing and sucking on the head of his penis, making him spasm once again. She giggled.

Alisha brought herself out of her memories to find herself at the door to his apartment. She began to smile, knowing that missing lunch for his sex was a treat in itself. He opened the door with a grin. She kissed him full on the lips before she crossed the threshold.

"Ready to eat?"

Putting In Work

She wanted to fuck, plain and simple. She didn't have time for love making; now was neither the time nor the place. Her meeting started in twenty minutes and she still had two reports to finish for the afternoon brief. She knew she should still be in her cubicle pounding them out, but this pounding she was getting from her boss in the storage closet was much more fun. Her morning was shot to hell and his huge dick thrusts and guttural grunts in her ear provided a much needed release. Nobody was working as hard as they should have been on this project except her so she decided, "Fuck them." She sent her a lover a quick text: "Fuck me."

They met in their usual spot, the storage closet on the 8th floor of their office building. This floor was largely underutilized and provided the perfect amount of discretion. Every few strokes he would put extra oomph in his thrust to try and get her to moan aloud. She knew what he was up to and she wasn't falling for it. His sex was good, but not that damn good that she was going to jeopardize her job.

None of that mattered right now, however. His erection sliding inside her and filling her juice-box was the only thing that held significance at this moment in time. He was long and thick, just like she preferred, and he knew how to use it. She braced herself against the wall with her back arched, her pussy getting wetter and wetter as she neared a mini orgasm. She pushed back against him, her ass bouncing against his thighs. He leaned back against the opposing wall to support himself, his balls slapping against her ass as he gripped her waist.

She lost track of time as he exploded inside her. She loved the way he came. It always pushed her into orgasmic oblivion. In fact, he was the reason she was on birth control. They never fucked outside of work but they fucked in the office often and he always came so much; she loved it. One of the added perks of having sex in the storage closet was the ample supply of toilet paper, sanitizing gel and paper towels.

He continued to slide in and out of her, his thick load of cum mixing with hers. Ounce after ounce erupted from the tip of his dick, his erection still invading her pussy. She was glad she decided on a skirt today: her pussy would be dripping his seed for another hour at least. He breathed a deep sigh, squeezed the rest of his cum inside her and pulled out before pulling up his pants, smacking her ass and walking out. There was always a ten minute window between their arrivals back in the office, plenty of time for her to clean up.

She didn't feel dirty; she didn't feel used. Actually, she felt rejuvenated. Sure, most would look down on their behavior, but she considered herself deserving for all the stress and bullshit she went through. She straightened her skirt and checked herself in her compact before heading out. She was going to nail this proposal.

Fantasy

He'd never met her in person, but that didn't stop his thoughts from wandering to erotic places whenever he thought of her, which was often. She haunted his fantasies. One moment submitting to his every perverse desire and in the next dominating his being.

He loved her sexuality, although she never displayed it blatantly. He'd met her online through mutual friends and fell in lust with her persona. Sure, she rarely spoke of anything sexual, but just seeing her picture drove him insane. Her lips looked so inviting, her skin so smooth. He wanted nothing more than to kiss her, tasting how sweet she was and finally realizing that yes, her lips were as succulent as they looked.

They talked online occasionally, but never to the extent that he truly wanted. He wanted to know that she wanted him inside of her as much as he wanted to fill her up. He checked his inboxes and message alerts often, praying that the day had finally come when she sent him a note saying that she had to have him and she had to have him now.

Days passed, weeks and months and all of his fantasies stayed to the side, unopened and unanswered. He satisfied himself with dreams of sucking on her, her nipples becoming stiff and her clit hard at his erotic inhalations. He could faintly imagine how wet she would be as he slid first one and then another finger inside her while kissing on her neck and breasts.

He wanted so badly to feel her hands teasing across his body, her full lips kissing across his chest. He grinned at the thought that he often thought of her while he was in the gym, patiently waiting for the day when he could showcase his hard work, all for her.

She wasn't the type to share personal photos or videos, but he constantly thought of how her sweet pussy might look. Was she a bright pink, a dull red? How wet would she get at his intense gaze into her love? He wondered if she would grab the back of his head with her hands as she pulled his face deeper and deeper into her or would she squeeze her thighs about him, making it nearly impossible for him to escape her orgasmic onslaught.

He knew that these were simply fantasies, but that didn't stop them from appearing with more frequency. He longed to be inside her. He'd seen pictures of her online and could imagine his dick sliding between her thighs, spreading her open for him. He wanted so badly to feel her nails digging into his back. He wanted to feel her lips kissing his, sucking on his tongue, moaning in his ear.

He continued to wait patiently, knowing that the day would eventually come if he could just bide his time. Until then, he stroked himself thinking of her breasts in his face, her nipples in his mouth. He envisioned her ass in the palms of his hands, massaging them while she lowered herself onto and off of his staff repeatedly. He knew the day would come when she would gasp in his ear as she came on him.

He turned on his computer, got online and continued to fantasize...

Whip Me, Strip Me, pt 1

She couldn't breathe, and she liked it. Joey's hands were wrapped tightly around her neck, his right thumb applying what could be seen as too much pressure to her windpipe. Her vision was blurry, her ability to focus on anything besides fighting for air slowly slipping away and yet she was having one of her most intense orgasms ever.

Denise wasn't into what you may call conventional sex and Joey loved that about her. His erection, long and hard, drove deep inside her as he continued to choke her. Her eyes began to roll into the back of her head and that's when he loosened up, but only a little. She took in a huge breath and looked at him with eyes raging with lust.

He turned her over quickly and slapped her ass hard, just like she loved it. She gasped aloud, a mix of pain and pleasure racing through her body.

"Harder!" She screamed as he pounded her pussy mercilessly, the sounds of their sex invading the air. He slapped her ass, again and again as she convulsed all over his dick, unable to control herself. He was hitting the right spot, both of them. He filled her completely and effortlessly, as they had done this dance before.

She looked back at him, her teeth bared, lusting for more. He leaned forward, never breaking stride and stuck a finger in her partially open mouth. She sucked on it greedily, slurping on his digit as if it were his dick instead. After she got it slick with her spit, he pulled it out of her mouth with a *pop* and slid it in her ass. She came instantly.

She loved it when he fucked dirty. Denise pushed herself further onto his finger and his dick, loving the feeling of being fucked simultaneously by two different parts of him. She couldn't help but shudder as wave after wave of dirty euphoria washed over her.

Joey used his free hand to slap her on the ass one more time before reaching up to pull on her hair. He gave it a sharp yank, causing her to gasp in pain, a pain that she relished. He continued to slide his finger in and out of her asshole, which sucked on him lasciviously, while driving his dick into her wetness, his balls slapping against her clit.

She was in heaven and everything that Joey was doing to her was divine. She wanted nothing more than to feel his seed erupt inside of her while she rode him hard. She wanted his level of pleasure to match hers. No, she wanted to exceed it and she knew what to do.

With a final push, Denise backed off of Joey's dick, albeit not without the slightest twinge of regret. She needed him back inside her, quickly. She surprised him by slapping him directly across his face. He wasn't expecting that, but he wasn't mad. He liked being the submissive one sometimes.

"Lay your ass down on the fucking bed." He did as he was told, switching places with her slowly, too slowly for her tastes, in fact. She pushed him back onto the bed, his head narrowly missing the headboard. She jumped on him like a tiger on its prey. "I said lay the fuck down!" She began returning the favors in which we initially found them, her fingers coiling around his neck. She wasted no time, immediately applying pressure while she slid down into his massive penis. She had to get as strong a grip on herself as she had on him, for she almost came, just like that.

Joey too enjoyed the asphyxiation, the thrill of losing control. Denise rode him like a pro; the feeling of slipping under consciousness mixed with slipping inside of her was almost too much to bear, but bear he did.

Joey managed to muster up enough control to reach around and lay hands on her back, running his nails from the base of her neck to the base of her spine. She shivered uncontrollably, beginning to cum on him yet again. Her pussy tightened on him, squeezing his erection as if she owned it. He exploded.

They came together, his cum spraying deep within her, flooding her walls until it spilled back out onto his shaft and balls. She continued to ride him, much like she was riding wave after orgasmic wave of ecstasy. Joey kept digging his nails into her back as she pumped her pussy juices onto him, his lap taking all of it. He pulled her close and pushed her ass further onto him as he continued to spurt his cum inside her, their juices mixing into cocktail of lust.

The weakness Denise felt after her last orgasm forced her to relinquish control of Joey's throat, which caused him to experience another, unexpected, orgasm. The pressure from his release surprised her, filling her with not just semen but also a blanket of pleasure. She leaned over and kissed him deeply, a romantic and brief reprieve from the heavy and violent session they just endured.

Once they came down from their sexual zenith, Denise reached under the pillow on the bed and pulled out a set of handcuffs. Joey was NOT expecting that...

Whip Me, Strip Me, pt 2

Joey tried fighting her off, but only a little. Denise knew very well that he was much stronger than her, but she was not going to be denied. She reached up and placed her hands around his throat again, a bit more forcefully than she intended. Oh, well.

"Stop moving, motherfucker!" She yelled at him, her eyes belying her true feelings. In reality she loved this cat and mouse game that they played during their sessions. It fueled the already flaming fire within her and filled her with randiness.

Joey did as he was told, unable to speak in protest, for she had tied a bandana around his mouth. She was especially kinky today and he loved it. Denise knew it as well, as she was sitting directly atop his stiff and determined penis. She wouldn't allow him inside her, however. She was going to torture him as much as she possibly could and herself in the process.

Denise looked over her work, pleased. He was bound and gagged, his hands handcuffed to the headboard and his feet tied to the bed's foot posts. She smirked, thinking that some of her friends would kill to have their men in a submissive position like this.

Joey looked so pitiful tied up like that, but the power she currently wielded turned her on immensely. She let her long hair trace innumerable fine lines from the top of his face and down his chest until her mouth was directly on top of his begging shaft. It jumped at her as her warm breath landed on it and she kissed it, the only merciful act she'd exhibited thus far. She wanted so badly to inhale his meat and devour him but she had to make him wait, right?

Joey was getting frustrated. His dick was aching and here Denise was, doing that teasing shit. He thrust his hips upward to meet her face, surprising her as his erection hit the side of her face. Her reaction was priceless and his muffled laughter filled the room. Denise stifled her laughter and slapped his leg, hard. Joey stopped laughing.

"Jokes, huh? You forget that you're the one tied up, sir." Denise let out a slight laugh as she ran her fingernails up his thighs to the point where his balls lay between his legs. He winced in pain, but she knew that he was immensely turned on. She looked down at his penis and saw the slightest amount of pre-cum leaking from his tip.

She reached down and stroked his dick hard, just like he does when he masturbates. She paused at the very tip to pinch him lightly. He jumped and moaned. She raked her nails up his opposite thigh as she continued jacking him off. She wasn't gentle, she knew what he liked. She leaned forward, the crack of her ass resting against his dick as she pulled first one nipple, then his other, into her mouth and between her teeth and bit down.

Her hand still behind her stroking him off, she continued to suck and bite on his nipples until she could feel his dick swelling with an impending orgasm, then she stopped.

Joey opened his eyes, pained at the sudden exit from contact. Denise got off of him and waited for the minutes to pass as his dick slowly went flaccid. Joey tried pleading with her through his eyes and mumbles through his gag but Denise wasn't having it. She enjoyed this torture session.

Finally, after he was slack and limp again, she went to him again, taking his balls into her mouth. She lifted up his cock with one hand, alternating between sucking on his nuts and massaging them with her other hand. She loved the way he tasted and felt, his dick so smooth and soft. Sexually, this was her favorite body part of his. She got caught up in licking up and down the sides of him, forgetting about everything else: the binds, the pain, the torture. She was in love with his sex stick.

She began using both hands to stroke him, squeezing his shank from base to crown and back again, her lips and tongue in hot pursuit. She turned herself around so that she was in a 69 position with him and began grinding her pussy on his face. Although she wanted so badly to stuff his face with her juiciness, she wanted to tease him more.

She continued pushing herself onto his mouth and face, driving Joey insane as he was so close to tasting her wet goodness and yet so far, her pussy hovering just centimeters away from his face. She sped up her tempo, sucking him harder and faster, professional in the way in which she sucked him off. Again, as he got to the very edge of a climax, she stopped. She looked back at him and could see the frustration and strain in his eyes. She liked that but she had had enough. She was horny and she needed to be filled.

She turned around and squeezed the base of his dick as she slid him inside of her. She leaned forward so that her clit was rubbing against the top of his dick, his lightly trimmed pubic area causing just the right amount of euphoria within her. She never allowed him to shave all of his hair off; she had too much use for it.

Denise debated taking the cloth off of his mouth, but she decided against it. She wanted to be making all of the noise today. She continued to grip tightly on his penis, delaying his orgasm until she got hers first. She knew that without restraint he would cum quickly, especially after what she'd put him through thus far. She teased him again by leaning forward and hanging her ample breasts in his face. She loved how helpless he was. She could see how badly he wanted to suck on her nipples, which were stiff and eager for a licking.

Her clit rubbed against him again, catching her off guard as she began to get increasingly excited. Abandoning all prior self restraint, she let go of his dick and buried her nails in his chest as she rode him hard, racing toward her penultimate orgasm. As she expected, Joey was already alongside her in their journey. The explosion of his semen inside her pushed her into sexual oblivion as he bucked his hips against her, resulting in sexual aftershocks. The waves of intensity crashed over her as she rode him for minutes afterward, their nectar mixing and running out of her and onto his thighs.

She leaned forward again as her kitty purred and calmed down, kissing and sucking on his neck, leaving her mark. She loved leaving hickeys on him, marking him as her territory. She rose up off his shaft, which was quickly losing intensity and slid back down. She repeated her motions, surprised at his dick becoming hard again. The sucking sounds of sex began to flood the room again. Damn, there was so much cum! She looked into his eyes, already glazed over, and contemplated another round.

Night of Debauchery, pt 1

The only thing I can think of as I walk to the hotel room is how badly I want to fuck you. Yes, fuck you. I don't want to have sex. I want to fuck. I want it gritty. I want it nasty. I want it to be hardcore. I knock on the door, my dick already jumping in my pants in anticipation, my body coiled to spring. As soon as you crack the door, I forcefully push it open, catching you by surprise. A shocked gasp leaves your mouth as you fall back and away from the door. Before you have a chance to compose yourself, I place one hand on the crotch of your jeans and grab a fistful of your hair with the other hand while slamming the door with my foot.

I push you against the wall, your hands barely having enough time to rise up in defense. You try to look back at me but I pull a blindfold out of my pocket and try to cover your eyes. You start to fight back, but it's no use. I'm bigger, I'm stronger and I am determined to get that pussy. I manage to get the blindfold on while still maintaining a grasp on your hands. You continue to struggle as I pull the handcuffs out of my pocket. You struggle even more so when you feel the first cuff click around your left wrist. In the scuffle, I manage to wrestle you over to the bed and throw you facedown. Your blindness makes it difficult for you to continue to fight me and walk at the same time so getting the second cuff on is much easier.

I pull my dick out, hard and raging, and slap it against your face. You try to turn away but it's no use. Your hands are cuffed behind your back and you've nowhere to run. I grab the back of your head and force my dick between your lips. Perhaps it's the resignation that you have no control over the situation. Perhaps it's the taste of my dick turning you on. Or maybe you just like sucking dick, but whatever the reason, you give in and open your mouth to receive me. I place both of my hands behind your head and guide myself into you slowly, filling your mouth and tapping the back of your throat. You make a slight gagging sound as I push. You purse your lips as I exit your mouth and enter again. I pull your hair hard as I begin to fuck your face, my balls slapping against your chin. I love this sight and am getting more and more turned on as you suck on me.

You're wearing a simple number, jeans and a t-shirt. I can see your impressive breasts through the collar of your shirt. I want to free them and feel your nipples in my mouth. I fuck your face harder and harder, your spit covering my dick and running down your chin and my balls. I'm so close to cumming and I want to hold back but I can't help it. The image of my black dick and your white skin and flushed lips is so fucking sexy. Without warning, I explode in your mouth, cum shooting to the back of your throat. You begin to gag and cough even more as my seed runs out of your mouth and onto the bed. You try to pull away but I hold you in place, making you stay until I finish cumming in your mouth.

Eventually I let you go and throw you back on the bed. You begin to thrash about, trying to get loose, but resistance is futile. Those handcuffs aren't going anywhere. I laugh at your attempts and begin undoing your pants. Unfortunately, your legs aren't restrained and I am unprepared for the onslaught of moving limbs. I sit on your thighs to hold you down and tell you to stop moving. You pay me no mind. Good. I rip open your shirt, your breasts wobbling in your bra in front of me. I feel myself getting hard all over again. I reach under you and unhook your bra, exposing your exquisite titties to me. I lean forward to take a breast into my mouth and smile as I hear you moan with pleasure. I can tell you're ashamed of yourself as you instantly try to get away from me again. I press all of my weight on you as I grab one breast in my hands and nibble, suck and bite on the other.

I flip you over after I manage to get your jeans unzipped and begin to pull your jeans down. Your kicking at me actually helps me get them off. Once the cool air hits your bare legs you attempt to slide off the bed and get away again. I pick you up and throw you back on the bed, your ass jiggling as I do so. I lay a slap on your ass after I slip out of my jeans. I get on the bed and straddle you again, pinning your legs down with my hips. I attempt to play with your pussy through your panties but your struggling makes it difficult, so I rip your panties off. I slide back just a little so that I can lift your hips off of the bed and bury my face in your ass. Obviously this wasn't expected on your part as you moan loudly and push your ass and pussy back onto my face. Once you regain your composure you try to get away again, but I have too strong of a grasp on your thighs, so you aren't going anywhere. I lick all over your ass and pussy, getting you nice and wet for me. You must know what is next because you increase your intense attempts at getting away. I'm glad that I brought those cuffs along; otherwise, this would have been extremely difficult.

I spit on your pussy, enjoying the way it makes you jump. My dick is so hard right now and I can't wait to slide inside. You manage to roll over on your back when I take my weight off a little, but it's no matter. I lift your legs up in the air and slam my dick inside you forcefully. The sudden invasion catches you totally off guard and I can see that you're caught between continuing to fight and giving in. The fighter in you says keep fighting, but my fighter keeps going as well. I spread your legs as I dig deep inside you, your struggles turning me on more and more. Your breasts bounce lewdly in front of me; mixed with your pussy sucking on my dick, quick work is made of me as I cum inside you. I increase my tempo as gallon after gallon of my juice seems to spill into you.

Despite the orgasm, I am still rock hard. I roll you over, my cum dripping out of your pussy and eye that asshole. I slide two of my fingers inside of you, coating them with cum before I slide them inside of your ass. You scream for me to stop because you know what is next, but I ignore your pleas. I line my dick up with your asshole, pressing against it slightly. Still wet with sex juice, I push against your rim, slowly easing it in. You continue to beg for me to stop, but that is just fueling my desire to take you, all of you. My knees are inside of yours, preventing you from closing your legs as I push further and further into your ass. I don't stop until my dick is buried in you to the hilt. I start to increase my tempo, my balls beginning to slap against your clit. Even your ass becomes wet as I start to fuck the hell out of you, the sounds of sex filling the room. I begin to pound mercilessly on your ass, your cheeks jiggling in front of me. I love the way your ass feels as it sucks on my dick and I fly over the edge again, this time cumming in your ass. I keep going, your butt draining me of all of my semen, until I am spent.

Once I've had my fill, I see your face beneath the blindfold, red and flushed. Hmm, I wonder how bad your revenge will be once I take the handcuffs off?

Night of Debauchery, pt 2 (The Revenge)

I'm still awake, watching the bruises on my thighs and arms as they form quite nicely. Not quite black and blue, but close. I sigh as I look over at you, sleeping peacefully. You really did a number on me and I have no complaints. I love it when we get rough and you definitely pushed me to the limit. Bravo.

You're not expecting retaliation, however, which makes the thoughts going through my head quite exquisite. You were so hell bent on crashing into the room and having your way with me that you didn't even notice the rope I had tied to both sides of the headboard. Good, you weren't supposed to.

I breathe another sigh, imagining that this is why some people smoke after sex. It just feels right. I move ever so slightly so as to not wake you, reaching for the cord at the farthest end of the bed. You shift just a hair and I freeze. I want this to be a surprise right until I get the last knot on you.

Leaning across you and I am so close when something catches my eye: the handcuffs! Oh, this is getting even better. They had totally slipped my mind, although now that I was thinking about them, a familiar soreness crept back into my wrists. They'll be a welcome addition.

I decided to straddle you, hovering just above your waist as I reach again for one cord of rope. I am thankful for my light touch as I ease your hand into the loop, tightening it just enough to hold you. Once you begin to resist, it will tighten on its own, doing the hardest part for me. You shift again just as I touch your other hand, your eyes barely cracking open.

In a daring move, I pull your second hand into the loop and tighten it enough to hold you just as your eyes break open. Your look is one of instant confusion as your hands are not by your side as you expect them.

"What the hell?!" You look around at both of your hands while I jump off of you and head to my night bag and pull out something. "What are you doing?" you ask.

"Returning the favor," is my only reply as I show you the cat o' nine tails I had recently purchased. Ooh, fresh leather. I smirk at the bug eyed look you're giving me now, knowing that you know exactly what it about to happen. Well, you don't know exactly, but I'm sure you have a clue. In case you don't, I bring the whip down across your naked thighs to give you a hint. Your howl brings an evil smile to my face.

"Now love," I continue," I am going to cuff your feet to the footboard, ok?"

"Like hell!" Another crack of the whip, another howl. "Ok! Ok!"

"Like I said, you're getting cuffed. And in case you hadn't noticed, your binds will only get tighter the more you resists, so be a good little boy, ok?" You nod silently. What else can you do?

After getting the cuffs on you, I feel the tiniest pang of guilt. This wasn't a part of this evening's plans and you were caught completely off guard. But then I remember my sore ass with your cum still oozing out. The guilt drips away. Anal sex, although very enjoyable and very fucking sexy, wasn't part of the plan either.

I go back to my bag and return with a silk bandana. I run it across your feet and up your shins and thighs, stopping a moment to swirl it around your manhood. He jumps in anticipation. I quickly move away, continuing on along your stomach and chest. I lean forward as if to kiss you on the lips and just as you reach up to meet my lips, I wrap the bandana around your eyes and head. Excellent work, I think to myself.

You groan, clearly not knowing what to expect next. I decide to tease you a bit by allowing my nails to walk a line from your nipples down to your manhood, this time giving you a few slow, solid strokes. As you begin to become aroused again, I take the very tip, only the tip, of you between my lips and suck, as if I am kissing a plum. That evokes another, more passionate, groan from you.

I stop almost as suddenly as I began, going to the other side of the room and gathering a candle that had been burning. I don't think you noticed that, either. I climb up on the bed, standing atop you and pour one...two...three drops of hot wax onto your legs. You jump in surprise, but helpless to go anywhere. I am so glad that you brought your cuffs.

"What the hell was that," you yelp. I jump down and growl in your ear, catching you off guard since you can't see where I am.

"Shut. Up. You talk again without permission and you'll feel a lot more than hot wax on your legs." I laugh inside as I hear you gulp. "As a matter of fact, I'm going to stuff your mouth right now." I get on the bed again, this time sliding my pussy across your mouth. "Eat," I demand.

You tentatively stick your tongue out, as if unsure of the directions. I grab the cat o' nine tails from the side of the bed and turn around, my ass covering your face as I lash you across the thighs.

"Eat my pussy like you mean it!" I honestly didn't know I had this in me, but this power is amazing. What's also amazing is the way that you suddenly attack my box, your tongue managing to find my clitoris before your lips start sucking on it. I lose my composure for a moment as I stifle a moan. I look down between my legs at you as I fight to stay upright. I grind myself down onto your face, my pussy juices starting to ooze down my canal and into your mouth.

This is a nice shift of power. I briefly look up to see your hands straining against the restraints, dying to grab my thighs and ass. I feel your tongue slide inside me, so I brace myself against your thighs as I move my ass up and down on your tongue, your flexible muscle licking out my pussy.

I look down and notice that you're rock hard again. I'm not surprised. I test myself and see if I can control my lust while still torturing you in the process. I lean forward to play with your balls while my pussy is still being gobbled up by you. I kiss and lick around your sack, doing everything I can to control myself and not touch your massive erection throbbing mere centimeters from my face. I decided to make a deal.

"If you want to feel my soft, warm lips around this heavy dick banging in my face, you better make me cum, and quickly." That did the trick as your tongue and lips go into overdrive, massaging, sucking and licking on my kitty with increased fervor. I bounce my ass on your face, making it a tad bit harder for you to get the prize.

You surprise me by flashing your tongue across my asshole on one of my downward strokes, causing me to lose my breath. You take advantage of the pause to devour my pussy. I start to shudder and shake as you attack my clit mercilessly, showing me who the true master is. I rise up involuntarily to find myself squirting all over your face and mouth. Oh, wow! I've never done that before!

My back arches as I squeeze on the closest thing to me, your dick, and my legs spasm out of control around your head. I can't believe how powerful this orgasm is as I fight to control myself. You lift your head up to me, continuing to suck on my clit while my love still rains down. I give in to the pressure and let the euphoria take over me, my clit being swallowed whole.

After what seems like an eternity of bliss, I finally come down off of my plateau. I look back to make sure you're not drowning in my cum and am met with a surprise. You're looking at me with the most deliciously evil grin. Somehow you managed to get out of my knots and take off the bandana. Oh, shit...

Our Mamasita

"Eat me while she sucks your dick." Heather lay back on the large bed as Tony kissed and licked her pussy, with Marisol at the foot of the bed inhaling his cock. The Brazilian moon crept through the open window and covered the three of them in an invisible sheet as their tryst began to pick up in intensity.

Heather and Tony had arrived in the land of the palm trees two days prior, both needing this vacation more than they could describe. Tony had just come from a year long stint in southwest Asia and Heather was celebrating the one year anniversary of her interior design business. It had been a good year for the two friends, but they were worn out and needed a break.

They'd met Marisol at a local dive, eyeing her across bottles of local beer before Heather made a move. Tony laughed to himself as he watched Heather approach her and whisper something in her ear before leading her out onto the small makeshift dance floor. He found himself mesmerized by the exotic moves that Marisol displayed, seeming to dance with Heather and Heather alone. He watched the two women as they slowly ground on each other, their faces mere inches from contact. It was no surprise that he was now rock hard.

Tony and Heather had been friends for years, but had never dated, never had sex, never so much as kissed. He was seeing her in a different light now. He could only imagine Heather kissing this strange and exotic woman as he nibbled on both sets of breasts between them. He couldn't believe the thoughts he was having, but he couldn't help it.

Tony snapped out of his reverie by the sight of Heather and Marisol actually kissing on the floor. The place was a favorite of the locals but was predominately empty tonight. The barkeep looked on lazily, possibly recounting the extreme days of his youth. He looked over at Tony as if to say "Aren't you getting in on that?"

Tony ambled over to Heather and their new found friend and grabbed them both by a hand to lead them out. Marisol grabbed a bottle of cachaca from the barkeep on the way out.

And now here they were, a liter into their bottle, clothes thrown about the hotel room and mouths busy at work. Heather had fantasized about getting it on with Tony for a long time, but never had the guts to say anything. She saw his head moving up and down as he sucked on her clit and she was glad that they waited. This all seemed so perfect. Marisol was trying her damndest to distract Tony and seemed to be making progress. Tony was no slouch in the meat department and Marisol was swallowing his staff like a pro.

After a few mini orgasms, Heather pulled Tony up and had him lean over her so she could taste his rock. She slid down so that Marisol could get a taste of her as well, and she dove in happily. Tony literally started fucking Heather's face, his balls slapping against her chin. He loved finding out about this raunchy, freaky side of her. He turned around to see Heather's legs wrapped around Marisol's head, pulling her further and further into her snatch.

He was on the edge of blowing his load when he opted for another position change. Lying on his back, he asked Marisol to straddle his face in the "69" position so that she could get some fun in as well. He didn't want her pussy feeling left out. He was so glad he decided on that one because he was amazed at how sweet her lower lips were. It was like eating candy! He was even more amazed when he felt a set of lips sucking on his erection and another one licking on his balls. He'd never had two women sucking him off at the same time before. He was momentarily distracted as he enjoyed the sensation.

While Tony was busy stuffing his tongue into Marisol's pussy, Heather was stroking him off with one hand and pinching Marisol's nipples with the other while alternating between sucking the tip of his dick and kissing her. She felt so high right now. She had needed this type of sexual release for the longest time, and now she finally had it. It was time to step it up a notch, however.

"You think you can handle sitting on his dick?" she asked Marisol in perfect Portuguese. In the moonlight, she could see her smirk and raised eyebrow, as if to say "Watch me" while she slid her ass forward to position her slit right above Tony's shaft.

The Backdoor

She loved it when he fucked her ass. He was calm with it, entering with ease and patience, as if his dick was massaging her gently from the inside. Other men always got so excited at the prospect of anal sex that they botched the entire process, so she only allowed him to have that foreign pleasure now.

And pleasure it was; he grasped her ass in both hands, lewdly spreading her open as he slid into her tight tunnel, the lubricant making the act that much easier and, dare he thought, sexier? He listened to her lazy moans fill the air as he placed inch after pleasure seeking inch inside of her. Her ass eventually swallowed him whole. She never failed to amaze him.

She grasped the sheets, her face contorted into a mask of ecstasy. It had taken her a long time to learn the secrets to successful sex in the most forbidden of regions, but once she began relaxing and enjoying the feelings, it was almost second nature. She exhaled with each push, relaxing her ass and allowing him deeper and deeper access.

He leaned forward after his cock had reached its limit and inhaled the scent of her hair. She always knew what turned him on and made sure to set every sense of his on fire. Her skin, so smooth and soft, played a wonderful companion to the essence flowing off of her hair and into his nostrils. Not taking his hands off of her behind, as soft as the sheets on which they lay, he began pulling himself out of her, stretching her even wider in the process.

She arched her back, unable to prevent her moans from becoming increasingly louder. She reached around herself to grab the back of his head, pulling him into her neck. He responded by nibbling along the length of her down to her collarbone. This was her beloved "spot," which caused her pussy to leak sexiness onto the bed. She reached underneath her stomach with her free hand and began to massage her clitoris with experienced fingers.

His tempo began to increase as her anal tunnel became more accommodating of his staff. He whispered sweet nothings in her ear that caused her brain to swirl just as much as her juices below. He kissed, sucked and licked along the expanse of her neck and back as he thrust into her before sliding out again, the lube and juices causing the sex sounds to engulf their matching grunts and moans.

He made her feel thoughts and emotions that no one else could and he did it with so much passion. She wanted nothing more than to feel more and more, and it seemed to come to pass with each orgasm that he blessed her with. She needed that now, craved to feel his warmth spilling into her body. She began to work and squeeze her muscles around him, knowing exactly what to do to get him off in the most exquisite manner possible.

He knew what she was doing and he was all for it. She was so comfortable with him and that turned him on in ways that no other woman ever could. The headboard began to beat a rhythm against the wall as he dove into her sex space repeatedly, racing toward a passionate finish. He was being helped by her fingers, alternating between playing with herself and kneading his balls as they slapped against her kitty. She had already had three or four mini orgasms and she knew she had more in store before the night was over. It was his turn.

With a final clench, she cooed "Baby, cum in meeee!" He responded with a breathless gasp as his manhood erupted inside of her. He clenched her ass as her ass clenched his dick, his fingers digging into her sweet flesh.

She loved every bit of it. She wouldn't relinquish her hold on him, determined to pull every ounce of sex out of him. She succeeded.

He collapsed on top of her, placing exhausted kisses along her backbone and shoulders. She wasn't worried, however. She began to expertly shake her ass, her cheeks rubbing and slapping against his defeated penis. It took only a few moments before his beast began to awake again...

About The Author

The Niftian considers himself a "geographical mutt," having spent considerable years of his early life in Kansas, New York City, and central Virginia. He began writing at an early age, showing a penchant for poetry and fictional short stories. During a stint in the military, he discovered a passion for erotic fiction and began pushing his works to the masses via his self created site at www.QuickiezOnline.com. He credits James Patterson, Zane, Nikki Turner, and Ken Follet as sources of inspiration. This is his first published body of work.

Connect with The Niftian Online:

Twitter: http://www.Twitter.com/The_Niftian

Facebook: http://www.Facebook.com/TheNiftianDOTcom

Tumblr: http://www.tumblr.com/TheNiftian

E-mail: TheNiftian@gmail.com

www.ingramcontent.com/pod-product-compliance
Ingram Content Group UK Ltd.
Pitfield, Milton Keynes, MK11 3LW, UK
UKHW040558210726
13854UKWH00008B/1385